Some Notes

on

THE GUIDANCE OF YOUTH

by DANIEL A. LORD, S. J.

◆

THE QUEEN'S WORK
3742 West Pine Boulevard
St. Louis, Mo.

Imprimi potest:

Peter Brooks, S. J.

Praep. Prov. Missourianae

Nihil obstat:

F. J. Holweck

Censor Librorum

Imprimatur:

✠ Joannes J. Glennon

Archiepiscopus Sti. Ludovici

Sti. Ludovici, die 6 Maii, 1938

Dedicated

to

Those Devoted Guides of Youth

The Men and the Women

Who Bind Their Lives

by Vow

To Serve the Sons and the Daughters

of Our Father in Heaven

SOME NOTES

ON

THE GUIDANCE OF YOUTH

❖

FOREWORD

These notes are an amplification of a course given during the summer of 1937 at the Sodality's Summer School of Catholic Action.

We make no claim that these notes cover the field of youth guidance. We do not pretend that they are even mildly technical. They are simply the observations and experiences of a priest who, by a series of happy and providential circumstances, has spent most of his active life working with young people. These notes are presented as some slight aid to those whose equally happy lot it is to work among the young Catholics in the present generation who are growing to manhood and to womanhood.

There is no greater privilege than that of working for young souls, who are so near to God. One comes to admire their faith, which is childlike without ever being childish. One comes to appreciate their brave and successful struggle for purity. One comes to sense their idealism, which they often take great pains to hide; one comes to realize their heroism, that needs only a small spark of inspiration to awaken them to magnificent deeds.

The modern young man (or woman) is much discussed and much flattered. Too much talk and too little sympathetic action have harmed him and made him self-conscious. Too many of the wrong people have spent too much time cajoling him; too few of the right people have given him enough help. He was born into an age that he did not make, and he has been nurtured amid the wreckage of standards and conventions that were being broken by other hands. He is puzzled by a world for which he is little responsible; he is troubled by a future that seems to be predetermined by forces which he neither evoked nor loosed.

Yet modern youth must be extremely dear to Christ. To modern youth a saintly Pope restored, just in the nick of time, frequent communion. And today the present Vicar of Christ summons youth to that glorious all-embracing extension of religion that we know as Catholic Action. Christ has been close to the young people of this generation. And He has great work to be done by the young men and young women who see the possibilities of their faith and its transcendent place in the world of here and now.

The Church has encharged her priests and religious to watch over and care for youth; to help youth toward the fulfillment of their possibilities of nature and of grace. But because the nervous vibrations that have been awakened in mankind by everything from the wailing of auto sirens to the roaring of big machines and the screaming of airplane bombs have wrought such swift changes in the outward seeming of youth, many a priest or director is more afraid of his charges than ever his charges could be of him. He loves them, but he is puzzled by them. He wants to help them, but he does not know how to go about it.

And from her cloistered safety, which even the busiest nun in the most active order enjoys, the sister in charge of young people regards her charges with bewilderment and approaches them almost diffidently.

And all the while youth waits for sympathetic hearts and understanding minds. Youth is lonely for the comfort that

FOREWORD

priests and religious men and women can give. Youth longs to talk but finds few listeners. Youth wants help; but though he gets plenty of abstract advice, few hands are held out reassuringly to him.

Young people—men and women, boys and girls—are far more anxious to be guided and counseled than is the most zealous priest or religious to guide and counsel them. They wait. They look up hopefully. Will they be answered?

Those who work for young people may be sure of a special place in the affections of Christ, the lover of youth, and of Mary, the mother of Christ's younger brothers and sisters. No other work takes more time than does this work for young souls. No other work requires more patience. But no other work keeps the worker younger, and surely no other work has a more far-reaching effect upon the future of the earth and of Christ's kingdom. Surely no other work is closer to the sacred hearts of Jesus and Mary.

This little book is respectfully offered to those men and women who help youth over the dangerous years to full maturity. It is laid in prayerful hope at the feet of her who is the mother of youth and of Him who is youth's elder brother.

The Octave of St. Raphael, Guide of the

Young Tobias. 1937

GUIDING THE MODERN YOUNG PERSON

The boy or girl, the really young man or woman of this particular year of grace—and I am writing this in the fall of 1937—is a mass of strange contradictions. He combines apparent sophistication with genuine simplicity. He knows so much about so many things and so little about so many more things, and often those many more things are the things it would be well for him to know. He is apparently so sure of himself, and yet in truth he faces the modern age with complete bewilderment. He seems quite certain that he can chart his own course; and in his heart he is so desperately lonely. He seems to resent intrusion into his private affairs; and he is so eager for the man or woman who can give him sympathetic understanding and common-sense guidance.

There is no slightest doubt in my mind that our modern young people really need correct guidance. Nor is there any doubt about their sincere desire for it. When they are confronted with big questions, when new and unexpected difficulties arise, when in their own bodies strange changes begin to take place, when they are faced with others' assertions that they know to be only partly true, when they run up against problems of conduct that demand solutions, young people realize with decided alarm that they have no personal experience on which to draw. They run to books, and the books confuse them only the more. Their associates give them half-baked advice, or treat the question with a wisdom that is transparently false, or brush the question aside with shallow contempt.

The young man or woman, notably the worth-while and serious young man or woman, wants to know the answers. And with limited experience, with misleading or difficult books, with companions no better equipped than themselves, where are they to turn?

Who will give them the advice and guidance they need?

The Parents of Today

The natural adviser and guide of young people is, obviously enough, the parent.

But for a variety of reasons—all of them quite intelligible—the modern parent does not advise and does not guide.

"Go talk to your father," I always used to say to the boy who came to me for advice.

"Ask your mother about that," I used to say to the girl.

The reply in both cases was an embarrassed look and then, in the great majority of cases, "I never talk to my parents about anything that's really important."

One can hardly put all the blame on the shoulders of the parents. Too many factors have got between them and their children. The modern father is by economic necessity an extremely busy man. He has to work hard to maintain the standard of living to which he has accustomed his family. He leaves the house early in the morning; he returns fairly late in the evening; he often has business engagements on Sundays and in the evenings; he feels that he owes himself a little recreation—a game of golf, a movie, a round of bridge or poker—on his brief holidays. And with a charming American casualness he has decided that "the children should be taken care of by their mother anyhow."

Many an American father wakes up one day to discover that his role in the life of his youngsters has become that of a bogey man. "Just wait till your father comes home; I'll tell him about this," cries mother, when things get past endurance. And father becomes a monstrous threat of vengeance held over the youngsters' heads. Even the fact that father is probably the mildest of disciplinarians does not much affect the case. Dad's role is that of a hobgoblin who snatches away from naughty children and rebellious adolescents their allowance, the hope of a new fur coat, the use of the car, a night out at a party, permission to go to the movies.

Poor dad!

And the modern mother is almost as busy as the modern father. Modern electrical devices were supposed to simplify housework and to give a woman plenty of time to spend with her children. Perhaps these modern devices do save time. But perhaps many of them are really time-consumers. Because she has an automobile, the modern mother no longer stands at the kitchen door and waves to the children as they start for school; she has to take the time to drive them to school. The radio brings her soothing music as she works about her house; but it also brings her programs to which she must give an attention undivided by housework. The gadgets of her kitchen and her general household have cut down her manual labor, but they have also increased her needs and the demands of her family. Simple pie must be supplemented by frozen desserts from the electrical refrigerator; the improved washing machine leads children to expect clean fresh clothes every school day of the year.

Demands have been made too upon the American woman's leisure. She has been encouraged to believe that she will be a better mother if she will give more time to self-development. And she believes it. But time given to self-development usually means less time that she can spend on the children. A modern woman with her clubs and lectures and courses and gym classes and beauty treatments and dentist appointments and card parties and charities and political interests is a pretty busy member of society. And the higher her standard of living, the more likely it is that she faces a daily program of staggering size and variety.

Anyhow the modern American public school has discouraged parents from taking an interest in their children. The attitude of many a modern pedagogue is that children are best off when the parents resign most of their claims in favor of the teacher. Parents, they say, do not do their children any real good. The education of the child will be competently and satisfactorily taken care of by the trained child-specialist—who in the majority of cases is unhampered and unprejudiced by any chick or child of his own begetting.

So, to eliminate the parents more effectively, the first grade was preceded by the kindergarten, and the kindergarten by the preschool; and now the preschool has its infantile prelude. I know of one school which admits pre-preschool pupils who have reached the robust age of two plus. For the teachers have solemnly agreed among themselves that they know all about the child and that the parents, who are only accidentally related to the youngsters, really do the youngsters a good deal of harm. And if teachers do not say exactly that, they do act on that theory.

It's not at all surprising then that the parent, seeing the elaborateness of modern education and hearing its efficiency praised to the stratosphere, decides that he probably is not the best influence for his little boy or girl. So he steps aside for the teacher and the psychologist and the child expert.

Many of the present-day parents suffer from another notable disadvantage: They are afraid of their own children. The modern educational system has trained the child to be brash and self-assertive. And the mother and the father are as a consequence intimidated. They cannot match their children wisecrack for wisecrack, and conversation becomes difficult when they pit their somewhat plodding minds against the slang repartee and pat replies of the child whom modern society has trained to the belief that he knows all the answers.

In addition the really generous parent wants to lift his child to a level higher than his own. At great sacrifice he gives his children an education far better than the one he had. Daughter comes back from college, wearing her collegiate hood with an air; and mother recalls that she considered herself privileged to have finished high school. Dad is vastly proud of his son, who goes from his university studies into a field of special studies; but dad recalls that his own education was full of holes plugged by the courses he took in the University of Job Hunting.

It's a good deal to expect a father and a mother to offer their hard-earned experience as a guide for boys and girls who have just stepped out of classes in experimental psychology and modern problems. If parents are today a little afraid of their own smart sons and daughters, it is because those same parents with sublime self-sacrifice have given those children advantages which have lifted them above their generous forebears. Their generosity has actually got between them and the possibility of knowing and helping their children.

There are certain questions too which a parent hesitates to discuss with his children. Any matter regarding sex immediately becomes personal when discussed by a parent. At least the parent thinks it does, and the result is embarrassment. The parent feels that if he discusses marriage, for example, the child instinctively thinks: "Oh, so that is the experience through which he has gone!" Parents believe that they cannot discuss love without betraying their own love experiences; that they cannot talk about the way in which children are born without creating in the mind of the child the immediate reflex: "So that's the way I was born!" For the parent the quizzical, questioning eyes of the child turn the impersonal talk on sex or sin or love into a highly personal self-revelation. And it is very likely that the child's attention to the talk has been purely impersonal. An understandable self-consciousness makes the father and mother think that the child's attitude is personal. And whether or not the parents are justified in their embarrassment, natural, easy confidence is destroyed.

Unless a parent starts to talk frankly and easily with his children when they are infants, talk on personal matters in later years is little short of impossible. It is very hard for the parent to explain to his children the experiences of love and marriage without his feeling that he is discussing his personal life and those sacred relationships in which both he and his children are intimately involved.

When the parent begins to talk to his children when they are very young, all is well. When the parent begins to talk to his children when they are in their adolescence, he is likely to get a bad case of stage fright and stammers.

And who are we to blame him?

For the plain fact is that it is always much easier to talk personally to strangers than to our own. If a complete stranger asks us for advice, we can give it without hesitation. The fact that we do not know the person too well removes all sense of being handicapped; we do not boggle over the fact that perhaps — maybe — possibly — we are giving bad advice to someone very dear to us. We are cool and objective and calm; we can see things in their absolute relationships. We are not troubled by any personal love for the person or by an intense desire to avoid even the slightest mistake.

Yes; it is easy to give advice to acquaintances and casual friends. It is easier to give advice and guidance to relative strangers. But it is extremely difficult to give measured, and objective advice and guidance to someone whom we love very much. Our very eagerness to help prevents our being natural. Fear thrusts its head in the way of calm counsel.

Love sees a hundred personal angles that complicate the problem almost beyond the possibility of solution.

God surely meant parents to be the guides of youth. Modern life, the modern school system with its self-confessed perfection, the educational advancement of each generation over the generation that bred it, parents' fear for their own children, parents' shyness in the presence of their own—all these things make the exercise of that guidance extremely difficult.

Happy the parent who begins to guide his children as soon as they understand connected words! And happy the children of that rare and splendid parent!

FALSE GUIDES

If the American parent is not going to fulfill his duty as guide and adviser of youth, there are plenty of people who will, who are volunteering to take his place. The trouble with these volunteers is that they are generally the wrong kind of guides.

The modern boy or girl, young man or woman, is surrounded by associates of his or her own age, associates who are more than willing to give information and advice. It's simply dumbfounding to realize how consistently wrong that advice is. It is of course information that is based on half facts and advice that is based on misinformation. Unguided themselves, they pick up scraps of knowledge in a fashion that closely resembles the methods of a scavenger. They get broken bits of information, often enough out of the gutters. They hear and misinterpret remarks made by their elders. They read, and they see neither meaning nor context. And without restraint or charge they peddle to their associates the resultant hodgepodge of old wives' tales, children's legends, false data, and snap-judgment conclusions.

The mass of misinformation that circulates among youngsters of all ages would fill set after set of encyclopedias. It's really a shame that someone with a taste for esoterica does not gather this misinformation in order to amuse or shock the mature reader.

Stimulated with the half information or the covertly communicated advice of his young companions, the youngster seeks fuller knowledge. He is shrewd enough to distrust his associates. Despite all the airs of wisdom that his companions assume, he realizes that they know little more than does he, whom they are "instructing" or guiding. Their information rings false. The data does not check with known facts. The advice sounds more than a little mad. And the youngster, instead of being helped, is simply precipitated into a frantic quest for real information.

So he goes scampering off for a book on the subject. Even if he gets a wholesome, sane, sound book, he may be unable to understand it. He is very like the amateur or the layman who dabbles with a medical book; the terms are strange and unfamiliar and to the untrained mind convey the wrong meaning. This dabbling is especially dangerous when the youngster picks up books on sex. For on this subject cold print, however delicately shaded, cannot but jolt and jar; the written word often seems so much more coarse and harsh than is the word spoken by a sympathetic person.

If however it is the youngster's bad luck to run into one of the guide books written by a pagan or by a man of evil mind, he is in a terrible way. All sorts of harmful texts are today offered to young people: texts on sex instruction, advice on love and courtship and marriage, treatises on all types of unmoral and immoral conduct, advice for the young man who is seeking a career or for the young woman who is hesitating between marriage, let's say, and some more spectacular form of life.

The writers of many of these books are atheists who regard man as no more than an animal. Their viewpoint on the most sacred relationships and indeed on the whole meaning of life is animalistic. They present solutions which ignore God and the decencies of Christian conduct. They write as if there never had been a divine teacher. They offer modes of living which exclude all consideration of the God-Man, who came that we might have life, and have it more abundantly.

Even if the young reader is not taken in by these professed guides and misguides, the fact remains that he is living in a world that is pagan and non-Christian. The neo-pagan attitude toward sex, marriage, love, careers, success and failure, the relative values of pleasure and happiness, the meaning of pain, the purpose of effort and labor—all this is written into the books that youth reads, the movies they see, the occasional plays that come their way, the songs they sing, the radio broadcasts they hear, the newspaper and radio commentaries on current affairs and popular *mores*.

Every writer today, whether he writes for the tabloid, the screen, or the encyclopedia, is a self-constituted moralist. Columnists who have risen from the status of vaudeville hoofers and have set themselves up as national recorders of the American scene analyze and explain life. The youngest cub reporter adds to his account of the latest divorce trial his own commentary on the social value of divorce. We are a nation of lecturers and propaganda writers, and sometimes I wonder whether young people are not the sole audience. We oldsters read and listen with our tongue in our cheek—after all most writers and lecturers address us with their tongue in their cheek. But young people have not as yet acquired the perfect technique of tongue-in-cheek, and they listen and read and are impressed.

CONSTITUTED GUIDES

Into this muddled situation comes the priest or the religious teacher, man or woman. To the problems of youth comes the conscientious lay teacher or the man or woman who has dedicated his life to the welfare of the young. Youth needs the help these teachers can give, the guidance and advice. What's more, youth wants that guidance and advice badly.

But for a dozen different reasons many of the best men and women hesitate; they are afraid to answer the call of youth.

We may as well begin with this clear fact: The priest and the religious teacher are natural and supernatural guides for youth. By virtue of their vocation they are the constituted guides of youth; to advise and help youth is one of the major duties of their state in life. Whether or not they will take up this work is not a matter of choice. The work is imposed on them by their vocation; it is part of their job. And if they fail to fulfill this duty, God Himself will one day hold them responsible.

PRIESTS

Pausing for just a moment on this matter of priests and religious teachers, we may as well admit with sorrow that this duty of help and guidance to youth is too, too often neglected. Especially sad is the failure of some priests to give advice and guidance in the confessional. There are some priests to whom the hearing of confessions becomes as automatic as the turning of the spokes of a turnstile. In and out, out and in; sins heard, absolution given; the slide opened, the slide shut; another confession, and another—absolution and penance, penance and absolution. If a doctor treated his patients with that sort of casual, automatic indifference, he would be barred from practice by the American Medical Association.

"Father," whispers the youngster, who has spent half an hour working up his courage to the point of confession, "I am guilty of self-abuse."

"Now you've got to stop that," says the priest. "For your penance you will say ten Our Father's and ten Hail Mary's, and go to Holy Communion."

He's got to stop it. That's precisely what the youngster already knows. But how? How is he going to break this habit that is tormenting his mind and making him nervous and furtive and terribly ashamed? The priest knows, from his moral theology, the remedies for self-abuse. He was taught in his pastoral theology how to apply these remedies to sinners. But for him the hearing of confession has become a semiautomatic process of granting absolutions. The boy leaves the confessional absolved, but he probably heads right back to his sin. Nobody has told him the methods of avoiding and eventually conquering his sinful habit.

"Father," whispers the young woman, "I'm in an office where there is a man who is an occasion of sin for me."

"Have you sinned seriously with him?" asks the priest.

"Yes, father."

"Is he married?"

"Yes, father."

"Well you have to stop that right away, or I can't give you absolution. For your penance say . . . and don't you dare do that sort of thing again."

The girl stumbles out of the confessional completely fogged, beaten, at an utter loss. The priest has made no effort to learn the circumstances of her sin. Does she need the job? Is she alone with the man during the day? Is it possible for her to avoid him? Where did the serious sin take place? Will it be necessary for her to give up her work? Can she easily find another position? Is she in love with the man, or is she only passionately tempted? A thousand elements may enter in. The priest should know these elements. It is his duty as physician to give advice. But he gives only a penance, a warning, and absolution, and he thinks he has fulfilled his obligation.

If the grace of God does not work in spite of this priest's neglect, the girl battles alone for a while, and then she stumbles back into sin.

God is going to have much to say to the priest who makes of his God-ordained profession a matter of automatic absolutions, who simply passes up his heavy responsibility of giving in the confessional the right and competent advice to those who come to him for it. He is guilty of serious neglect of one of the important duties of his state in life.

RELIGIOUS TEACHERS

I find it hard to forgive the religious teacher who is too busy with Latin or literature or mathematics or science or history, too busy to remember that he or she has a prior obligation to be the guide of souls. The religious who is too busy with classroom material to watch for a chance to help young people with their personal problems might just as well take off the habit or the cassock and go teach in a school where soul guidance is not part of the normal duties. To teach a subject magnificently is to do only half the job. The religious teacher must guide the youth he teaches, must take an interest in the personal problems of his students.

Students complain bitterly of the failure of their religious teachers to be in the slightest degree concerned about them.

A young lady who was soon to be graduated from a famous Catholic girls' college gave the sister dean a competent dressing down—in my presence:

"You and the other sisters are splendid religious. You are fine teachers. We admire you, and we respect you. But

I came to a Catholic college because I hoped for much more than that. I wanted your friendship and your sympathetic guidance and your help. And what happens? When the class is over, the sister picks up her books and retires to the holy precincts of her cloister. You are on the job when there is a matter of class work or schedules or grades or credits to be handled. You disappear when such things are attended to. But it is outside the classroom that the real problems of us young women begin. I came to college for the companionship and friendship and sympathetic guidance of nuns, and you nuns have failed me."

The young woman later became a nun of that very order, so she cannot be accused of having had a grouch or a prejudice. But she entered the novitiate with a vowed determination that when her time came to teach she would give to the students under her a little of her time, much of her love, and a great deal of patient attention and understanding.

If women religious sometimes fail in their duty, men religious fail more notably and more frequently. They are absorbed in a thousand things. And men students and boys in our Catholic schools complain bitterly and with apparent justification that "nobody cares."

The president of one high-school senior class said to me: "I'm not going on to a Catholic college next year." I protested, but he was firm: "What's the use? I've been in this Catholic high school for four years, and nobody on the faculty gives a damn about us."

He was cynical; and he evidently felt that he had some reason for his cynicism.

There are, I know, religious teachers who could and would do marvelous things for their students but who are held back by the reluctance or the actual prohibition of their religious superiors.

Being a religious superior is certainly no easy job. In any community there is every possible grade of tact and talent. Some have the gifts of real apostles of youth. They can go straight to the hearts of young people and can open those hearts to God's grace. There are the great majority, who can do important things for young souls, who have a normal sympathy, honest love, zeal, and good intentions—all of which is supplemented by the willing grace of the Savior. There are the bungling ones. These may be ever so well-intentioned, but they bruise the souls they touch, and when they are given a confidence, they hardly know what to do with it. Then there is the rare case of the unusual religious for whom almost any personal contact with souls is a problem and a peril.

Now the terrible danger is that superiors, running into that last unhappy, unusual religious, may get a bad attack of nerves and forbid everyone in the community the ordinary work for young people. We can take it for granted that religious superiors are appointed because they are supposed to have better than ordinary sense. How absurd, then, if they permit their conduct toward all the members of their community to be dominated by the failure of any one member!

The religious superior knows that his or her community is consecrated by God to the work for young people. The talented and the apostolic must be actually cheered on in their work for young people. The ordinary, good, normal members of the community must be given the highest possible encouragement in their devotion to their students. The bungling ones can be trained. Bungling is by no means incurable, and one of the really important jobs of the superior is to eliminate, not the bungler, but the bungling of the bungler. Instead of personally dealing with young people, the first job of the superior is to help the members of his community in the work they are doing for young people.

If there is unfortunately a fool in the community, well—
fools must be protected from their own folly. When a religious regards work for young people as dangerous to himself,
the wise superior takes the wiser course: he or she shows that
religious how to avoid the danger.

It is so easy, so exasperatingly easy for us to issue
sweeping orders. We find it simple to control the folly of
the stupid by issuing a general mandate of veto that cuts
away the work from the vast majority, who can do and are
doing wonderful things for souls. Work for young people is
in the overwhelming majority of cases neither perilous nor
dangerous nor even remotely an occasion of sin. The fact
that some unusual or abnormal person finds it so is no reason
in the world for barring the normal and wholesome religious
from the work to which they have consecrated their lives.

Stupid indeed is the superior who forbids the young
religious, the very ones who can be most powerful in their
influence over young people, to have any real contact with
youth. It is plainly absurd for superiors to grow actually
excited when they find a teacher giving time and thought and
attention to students. Sad, unfounded, and frustrating are
the suspicions aroused in certain superiors' hearts by the
popularity of a teacher, when all that that popularity means
is that the teacher is sympathetic and interested in his or her
pupils.

Superiors are thwarting the work of God when, because
of the stupidity or folly of some misguided individuals they
know or knew or heard about, they issue large and sweeping
orders, such as: all classrooms must be cleared immediately
after class; students are to be cared for only by a chosen
few faculty members—usually old, unattractive, and unsympathetic.

Superiors sometimes erect barriers between the religious

on their faculties and the young people, whose tuition has been paid in the hope that they would receive the personal guidance and help of those religious. Superiors, guided by all sorts of motives, have been known to lace into young religious who work heart and soul for boys and girls, to voice suspicions of the virtue and the motives of these religious. Perhaps because of the mistake of one stupid or misguided individual, superiors sometimes establish a sort of tradition for their schools: that the faculty must be insulated from the student body, lest sparks fly and a fire ensue.

Well an examination of conscience should quickly show any superior who takes an attitude like this that he or she is cheating the religious on the faculty of their finest work and their noblest careers. He or she is cheating the students of the very thing for which they rightfully look in a Catholic school.

What superiors should really worry about is, not the popularity of a religious teacher, but the presence on the faculty of those teachers who are not at all popular with the students. Superiors should grow alarmed when they do not see the faculty and the students, the individual members of that faculty and individual students who need help, in close association. Superiors should look quizzically and suspiciously, not at the teacher to whom the students throng and flock, but at the teacher who has no friends among the students and who rushes from class through silent lines of boys and girls to spend the rest of the day in his or her private room—yes, or even in the chapel.

If superiors ever get rid of a teacher because that teacher is popular with young people, if ever they lay down laws that prevent the free approach of students to their teacher, if they object to a decent and wholesome interest of the faculty in the students, if they do not actively and sympathetically encourage the members of their community to help their students—even at the sacrifice of time and, if need be, the perfect regularity of the community routine—then God is, I feel, going to hold them seriously accountable. They are getting between their religious and the God-appointed duty of these religious. They are thwarting the work for souls. They are keeping the shepherds from their sheep. They are turning a teaching order into an order of hermits and contemplatives.

Yes. It is true that some individuals are indiscreet and unwise. And that is precisely the point. Some individuals. How rarely does it happen, though, that people are indiscreet and unwise through zeal! They are much more likely, human nature being what it is, to be indiscreet in their avoidance of the difficult task of youth guidance. They are much more prone to be lazy, aloof, and unsympathetic. Handle these individuals. Don't penalize the faculty. Don't put a stop to the zeal of the community.

If being indiscreet with youth really means being sinful with or dangerous to youth, superiors may well take precautions. But as people grow older, they are sometimes inclined to mistake zeal for indiscretion and laughter and merriment for unwisdom. I doubt very seriously that God will allow evil to befall a religious community that is dominated by zeal for souls. Superiors will do well to watch out for apathy and laziness and a dodging of responsibility with quite as keen an eye as they watch out for indiscretion and possible danger.

With faith in God and zeal for His interests religious can keep evil out of their community; with faith and zeal religious will not avoid doing good for souls for fear of possible evil. Better to inspire a community with a real love of souls and a real zeal for the happiness of those young people entrusted to them than to fulminate laws that cut off love and guidance and sympathy from Christ's young people.

I myself have never met a religious that I thought suffered spiritually as a result of devotion to young people. I have met many whose neglect of young people was a clear sign of a lazy, "zealless," selfish soul. I have never found a superior that encouraged his or her religious on the faculty to work for the students and be close to them in understanding and interest who was not a broadminded and intelligent person with a Christlike heart and a vision of His work. I have met a religious superior who cut the faculty away from sympathetic association with the student body, but that superior was a Jansenist at heart, unfit to be in charge of an institution whose purpose was the preparation of souls for the loving Christ and for the work of advancing His kingdom in the world. If people are going to be kept from doing their duty because of fears and manufactured conventions and scruples, how is the work of God ever to be accomplished?

I may as well say, in closing this unpleasant subject, that the superiors who interfere most with the work of God by preventing their faculty members from working for and with young souls are far more frequently women than men.

LAY LEADERS

During the past few years more and more lay leaders have been introduced into the work of our schools and our youth movements. That is splendid. Young people often derive a certain consolation from seeing lay men and lay women in this apostolic work. And these young people can on occasion talk to the lay person more easily than they can to the religious.

By the fact of their presence in a school or in a movement devoted to young people, these lay men and lay women are commissioned, within reason, to be the guides and counselors of souls.

Much, very much of what I have said and shall say of

priests and of religious teachers holds for these lay teachers and leaders.

ATTITUDE TOWARD CONFIDENCES

So with listening heart and sympathetic mind the guide of souls approaches the glorious task of helping young people solve their problems and face their difficulties, be those problems and difficulties in the natural or in the supernatural order.

That task is plainly a duty. It is also, incidentally, the source of deep personal satisfaction and joy.

The first simple rule in the matter of the confidences of young people is this: Confidences can be neither coaxed nor forced. The worst possible approach that the zealous elder can make is to greet the younger person with an ingratiating smile and say: "Now sit down and tell me all about yourself."

If one knows the young person well, such an approach may be the correct one. It may be best to take the matter firmly in hand and say: "Let's get this thing settled once and for all."

But generally it is fatal for a merely well-intentioned person to beg or to ask for or to seem to expect the confidence of a young person. If the young person is even normally shy, he will run a mile and protest all the way that he has nothing to talk about. If he is brash and sophisticated, he is likely to sit down and reel off a line that will burn the ears and blister the skull of the oldster. The oldster was looking for something, and the youngster was loathe to disappoint him. If the young person has nothing to tell, or if he has no intention of pouring his confidences into this particular ear, he'll spin a yarn just the same. And a magnificent act by a youthful Munchausen is the result.

To go about looking for confidences is to become ridiculous, and eventually the youngsters run like scampering hares when they see the confidence-stalker approaching.

Confidence and confidences come to the person who earns them, and to no one else. We do not ask for confidences; they are given to us. We cannot seek out souls that need help, or rather we cannot seem to be seeking such souls. They must think that they are coming to us because they themselves chose us and because they recognize us to be the possessor of an understanding heart.

Confidence and confidences are earned quite simply. They come to that man or woman who has shown a genuine interest in the youngster.

No matter what the age of the young person, he or she is quick to recognize the person who sincerely likes him. The young person senses that older person's interest for youth in general. He senses the fact that the older person feels a personal interest in him as an individual. The invisible antennas of a youngster are extremely powerful. Those antennas he unconsciously stretches out in the hope of finding someone who is interested in young people and believes in them; and when his antennas further report the fact that this particular person likes him as an individual and is willing to give him attention and sympathy, a contact is established that is the prelude to confidences.

I remember a certain young man religious teacher who was loudly lamenting his failure with young men. He had a class of seniors in high school, and he admitted that he was making no headway with them.

"I don't know what's the matter," he said, in a sharply rising voice, "but I can't get any place with the dirty little brats."

That was just the point. He was seriously trying to work for them. But when he first walked into the classroom, they saw the mental epithet "dirty little brats" written across his face. He might really try to do his stern duty by them with highest motives and real disinterestedness; he would never get their confidence. They knew he disliked them, and they shied away from his duty-prompted devotion to their interests.

On the other hand, when a man or a woman really likes young people, nobody, least of all he himself, has to advertise that fact. The young people sense it. They come to him willingly and readily. And when a boy or a girl sees interest and sympathetic understanding in the eyes of an elder, words are quite unnecessary, and actions can be delayed. The youngster knows his friend and on his own initiative takes the first step toward the listening heart of that friend.

Perhaps one of the first tests to which a young person puts his friend is this: "Is he willing to give me time?" The oldster who sits talking to a boy or a girl and keeps one eye on his wrist watch is simply choking all confidence. A little later in the book I am going to take up the matter of the circuitousness of the route by which all young people come to speak of the subject nearest their heart. The way to a man's heart may be through his stomach; the way to a boy's —and to a girl's—heart is all the way around the bush.

So all young people watch to see whether or not those who profess to be interested in them are willing to give them time—time to talk, time to listen, time to answer their letters, time to discuss their aims and ambitions, time to thrash out their difficulties. The confidant of youth must banish time from his mind, at least so long as he is with the young. Young people have all the time in the world ahead of them. They resent the attitude of "Come on, now; let's get this over with. State your case briefly, and let's be about important matters." You don't blame them, do you?

Honesty is a great asset. And young people like their advisers to be honest. The young person is bored and annoyed by the faking and stalling of an adviser who is trying to cover up the fact that he does not know the answer to a question. The youngster is frankly impressed, however, and really pleased when the adviser says: "That's a question I can't answer just now. Give me time to look it up or to think it over. Come back tomorrow, and I'll try to answer you then." The young person is glad to deal with someone whose fund of information isn't quite encyclopedic; too much wisdom and too much pat data pulled out magicianlike sometimes disturb and annoy the young person. He does want honesty, and wants it sincerely. That is why an honest admission of ignorance impresses him favorably.

Honesty is shown in a willingness to face any question. The guide should not dodge one question with the answer to some other question which was not asked. Youngsters know that trick. They themselves have used it at some time or other during an examination; they themselves have answered some question other than the one asked, hoping that the teacher will think they misinterpreted the question. So they are bored when the older person uses the same trick with them.

They are roused to admiration when the honesty of their friend entails a personal sacrifice. "Yes," says the guide, in answer to a personal and, to the youth, an embarrassing question, "I quite understand. I went through something like that myself." That's an honesty that impresses and pleases. The adviser may with safety even confess to temptations against purity. Sometimes it is wise for the guide to admit that he or she has at various times been subject to many of the common temptations of mankind. It is not, however, wise ever to mention personal sexual sins to young charges. That shocks. More than that; it sometimes makes the youngster feel: "Well, if he did it too, I guess it really can't be so bad after all."

SILENCE

One of the greatest endowments of a guide or an adviser of youth is the great gift of silence. Confidence responds to attentive silence as it does not respond to eloquence or wisdom. The young person enters the room of an adviser. He sits down nervously. The adviser talks briefly of a dozen different things—the weather, sports, movies, mutual friends —and then quietly, with an imperceptible decrescendo, subsides into silence. The youngster fumblingly begins to talk. The guide is flatteringly silent; he apparently wants to listen so that he won't miss any important point.

Good counselors are not necessarily good talkers. But they are good listeners. It is not with the prod of much speech that they stimulate confidences. It is with the compliment of attentive listening that they draw out the speaker. I shall treat this point at greater length later on.

One thing that kills confidences absolutely is any resentment on the part of a director when he learns that one of his charges has confided in someone else.

I know of cases in which counselors—priests and men and women religious—were helping and advising many young people and were getting along splendidly; then the counselors found themselves losing face with their groups. The line before their door grew thinner. They found the boys and girls friendly but uncommunicative. Often they never discovered the real reason for the change. Somehow the students or the youngsters learned that the counselors put on a scene when some other priest of the parish or some other member of the faculty occasionally advised these young people.

"Taking care of these kids is my job," stormed the counselor in one instance, "and I want you to keep your hands off."

Young people have no respect for an oldster who is not shrewd enough to know that people must choose their confidants. Youngsters are smart enough to know that the counselor who resents confidences given to anyone but himself is really conceited. They realize that he looks on confidences as being his by right; that he collects them as someone else might collect stamps or matchbox covers. And when youngsters realize all this about a counselor, they stop going to him—and often they don't start going to anyone else. They decline to be fought over. They are resentful that their confidence, which they quite properly regard as theirs to dispose of as they please and to whom they please, should be claimed as the exclusive right of any one man or woman.

Need I say that among both men and women this type of counselor is not rare enough? Communities and parish houses are split wide open by a priest or a brother or a nun who is furious when a certain young person does not follow his usual custom and confides in someone else.

"I direct the vocations in this house, and you'll be pleased to mind your own business—which is not the young people."

Just let that attitude become known to the youngsters, and they keep their counsel to themselves. They won't be the center of an undignified struggle. Bless 'em for it!

TECHNIQUE OF CONFIDENCES

Once the young people know that a priest or a religious or a lay guide is interested in them, confidences may be given at any time or place. I know one student counselor who spends the entire recreation period on the edge of the playing field. He finds that young men talk easily and personally when they are relaxed and in the atmosphere of watching a not too exciting game. He plays with the young men—he bats out flies and kicks a ball around. And frequently when he is walking back to the house, some young fellow joins him and starts to talk.

I have always felt that the most unusual spot in which a confidence has ever been given was where one was given me—backstage and near the electric-light switchbox. A priest friend of mine and I had built, as an experiment in stage-craft, the sets for a college production of "As You Like It." Dressed in rough clothes and a sweater, I was presiding at the light box during a matinee performance of the play. Suddenly I looked up and saw standing near me the young woman who was playing Rosalind and who had just emerged from the Forest of Arden. She was the outstanding leader at the college, no doubt of that; she was good looking, highly competent, and had brains and abilities in a dozen different fields.

She hesitated on the edge of the forest for a moment, hose and doublet—costume for the forest scene—dark against the glare of the stage lights.

Then suddenly she turned to me and said, "Do you think I could be a nun?"

I must have gasped—I was still very young—for she grinned and hurried on.

"Well whatever you think, I'm going to be a nun." And then in a burst, "But if you dare tell anybody, I'll half kill you."

By that time I had regained my breath.

"Of course you'll make a glorious nun," I said. "Congratulations." And then I laughed. "But honestly, I'll bet that no vocation in all history was ever announced in a more weird spot or in a more incongruous costume."

She became a successful nun, and a successful nun she is to this day.

If, however, one is seeking the ideal place for confidences, I should say that confidences are most frequently given when and where the confider is at ease. That is the reason why many smart guides of youth see to it that the rooms in which they meet young people are very comfortable and more than a little attractive. Father Cornelius Shyne set a sort of standard when at Georgetown Preparatory in Washington and later at St. Louis University High School he furnished the student-counselor's room with comfortable chairs, beautiful pictures, good rugs, and generally created an atmosphere of leisurely ease. Father Ronald Knox receives the Oxford undergraduates in a grand old beamed library, where a fire burns comfortably all day and all evening and where the Oxford student may stretch out in a deep chair and smoke a cigarette or a pipe.

Physical ease, however, is only a symbol of the mental ease that precipitates confidences. When the young person is relaxed, because he or she is either physically comfortable or mentally reassured, conversation is easy and confidences flow. An easy and friendly air on the part of the older person is important. There must be no slightest tension in his attitude. A preliminary desultory, friendly chatter calms nerves and relaxes tenseness. The immediate first question is often fired from so tense and so taut a youngster that you can hear the twang of the bow as the arrow of the problem is shot at you. But if the director wants further confidence, something beyond the first winged question, it is well for him to see to it that the young person is physically comfortable and mentally at ease.

ALL AROUND THE BUSH

I have previously suggested that the young person's approach to something really personal and important is all around the mulberry bush. The longest way home is the shortest way to his problem. There is a first approach, a windup, a preliminary shot or two, a running up to the hurdle and a shying away—all before the real subject is reached.

The young person will talk perhaps for half an hour in order to work up courage to broach the subject of his problem. That is why it is so necessary to be willing to give time. He or she will talk about the people at a recent party he went to; about the funny thing that happened in class or at the office; who is dating with whom and why; about a book he has been reading or a play he has seen; about a new enthusiasm or a new acquaintance. . . . And then he will suddenly lapse into silence. The question is now at hand.

We must remember that young people distrust, and rightly distrust, even their friends. They are never sure of the reception that will be given their problem. So they bury really important things in a mass of distracting and harmless detail.

When a young person, a boy or a girl, has something really terrifying or embarrassing to tell in confession, that something is almost never told at the beginning of the confession. He or she does not say: "Father, I burned down an orphanage with all the orphans in it." He or she says: "Father, I was slightly disobedient to my parents, and I wasted time, and I was careless about my prayers before meals, and I omitted my morning prayers three times, and I was uncharitable . . . (a brief pause, and then a sudden burst) "and I burneddownanorphanagewithalltheorphansinit . . . and I was unkind to my little brothers and sisters."

For some reason young people feel that if they sandwich the important "crime" in between a mass of frivolous or trivial details it will pass unnoticed, or, at worst, will be treated with a light touch.

Now when there comes that brief preliminary pause which indicates that the young person has reached the really important subject, the director should recognize that he has been given a cue. The pause itself may be the cue. Significantly it may continue longer than one would deem necessary. So the older person says, in a very matter-of-fact way, "Something on your mind?"; or "If ever you'd like to talk to me about any problem, I'd feel complimented"; or "Something bothering you?"

An unwise comment would be: "Something seems to be bothering you lately." A very close older friend might say that if he was sure that the young person's reaction would not be: "Oh! I've been so obvious about my problem that people are noticing me." But unless one knows the young person extremely well, it is not wise to suggest that his problem has become a thing that the man who runs can read in his face.

UNINTERRUPTED STATEMENT

The smart director lets the young person talk without interruption. Ten to one, if the problem is a difficult one, the youngster has rehearsed his statement of it down to the last comma. He has mentally phrased it so that when spoken it will be clear and intelligible yet as innocuous sounding as possible. He knows just the inflections he will use, just the gestures that will accompany his words. He may not even be aware of how well rehearsed he is. He wants to feel that he will give an honest statement and a clear one, a statement that will not involve him too much—either in appearance of guilt or in commitment to some future course of conduct.

Now if the director interrupts with a question or a remark, the young person's well-rehearsed monologue is thrown out of line. The boy or the girl has to start all over again and is a little embarrassed if he finds himself repeating the identical words and phrases that he had used in his first statement; he becomes confused if he has to grope around for new words and phrases in which to couch his story.

Besides, the priest's or the nun's interruption often has no bearing on the case. Having heard only part of what the youngster has to say, the director has formed what is perhaps an entirely incorrect impression. The questions which the director asks may concern something which the youngster intends to make clear somewhat later in his rehearsed recital. Interruptions are usually a mistake. Save questions and comment until the end.

I well remember a young fellow who sat in my room in a sweat. He had something dreadful to tell me. He began a rehearsed story. It was about something shameful. It concerned others. Quickly my mind jumped ahead and saw the worst. Clearly I was dealing with a lad who had got himself into a bad mess, probably something connected with sex. My inclination was to ask questions, to interrupt, to begin giving wise advice. Some guardian angel, mine or the boy's, held me back. I remained silent.

Then as he continued to talk the truth dawned on me. The shameful thing he wanted to talk about, the thing that concerned others, was the fact that he had been borrowing book reports from other chaps. I almost laughed aloud in my relief. But I thanked God, who had kept me from making a fool of myself and from completely dumbfounding and disturbing a remarkably saintly soul. Suppose, while the youngster was struggling with that common youthful felony, a cribbed book report, I had interrupted with questions or sage advice about sex. It was a lesson for me, and I pass it on.

There are intervals during a youngster's recital when a little gentle prodding may be needed. As the recital slackens, the listener can say, "Yes. I see"; or "I understand"; or "You've made that all perfectly clear; go ahead." Anything that indicates that the problem is being grasped and followed may help the narrative.

But it is quite possible to talk oneself out of confidences. I ran across a student counselor who became a bit of a joke. The minute the young person began to talk, the wise elder cut in with: "Yes. I understand just what you're talking about. I had a case once of a person who . . ." And bingo! The garrulous elder plunged into the recital of somebody else's story, which bored the confider, threw the prepared narrative completely out of line, and finally dried up all possibility of confidence. The young person had come to talk, not to be given anecdotes. And the gush of the counselor's talk got between the counselor and the important problem to be discussed.

When there is nothing to say, don't say it. That's the good rule. And when a young person wants to talk, until he has said his full say and stopped, there is nothing, absolutely nothing for the oldster to do but listen.

Shock-Proof

Anyone who is dealing with young people should of course be shock-proof. Any sign of disturbance or surprise or disapproval in the director is fatal to confidence. Either of two things happens: The serious and well-intentioned young person is thrown back into deep despair, or the frivolous and excitement-seeking person has achieved his end. I know one volunteer guide in whom young people confide for the sheer joy of seeing her shocked. They tell her the most ghastly stories. They embroider for her the most alarming tales. They run to her when they have returned from parties and give her accounts of what amount to orgies—just to hear her "Oh!" and "Ah!" and "Tut-tut!" and "My dear, you really couldn't!" They have a perfectly grand time with her, and it causes them endless amusement.

The person who tells a sordid tale that is true watches with keenest perception for reactions from the listener. The speaker has a sense of degradation. Shame envelopes him. He is convinced that anyone who hears the tale will condemn him. Worse; decent people, he has decided, will shrink from him and feel involuntary revulsion. The young person who comes to discuss some unpleasant habit or action half expects to see the cassock of the priest or the habit of the religious drawn away from him and the lips of the listener curling in instinctive scorn. He expects that reaction, and yet he dreads it.

So even though his eyes are lowered while he is speaking, he is watching and waiting for the chill or the hot blast of disapproval and scorn. The chill does shake the listener. Hot resentment or indignation flashes for a moment in his eyes. The poor youngster wants to crawl into some small hole and die. Indeed his confidence may end right at that point.

So any man or woman who expects to deal effectively with young people must school himself or herself to being shock-proof. As the youngster talks, no sign of shock or disap-pointment or surprise must mark the listener's attitude. And certainly the director must show no irritation or displeasure, for if he does, the whole thing ends.

For one thing, who are we oldsters that we should act toward young people as if their wrongdoing was directed at us personally? The one who is hurt by sin is God, and He is tender and merciful. The reception which Jesus Christ gave to the returning Peter should be typical of the attitude of any guide, especially the guide of youth. Christ, we recall, did not so much as refer to Peter's triple denial. He merely gave the repentant Apostle a chance to say three times that he loved the man he formerly denied three times.

One must listen to any story or recital in the calmest

fashion possible. One has to school oneself to showing no reactions, except the pervasive reaction of continued and growing interest.

Sometimes it will happen that the young person himself interrupts his or her story. (How we all wish, by the way, that there were some pronoun that stood for both him and her; this constant effort on my part to include both the boy and the girl in my discussion may be as annoying to the reader as it is difficult for my grammar.) Sometimes the young person cuts into the recital with: "I suppose you are frightfully disappointed"; or "I guess you're badly shocked, aren't you?"

Never will the wise guide admit that he is disappointed or shocked. Surprise and shock have no place in the director's reactions. The director's answer, even if he is shocked or surprised, should be an evasion: "You've had a hard problem, haven't you?"; or "You've certainly been through a tough time, and I'm sorry." The reply to a direct question should be sympathetic and kind. We must remember the essential heroism that lies back of a frank confession of a sad and sordid story. It takes grit on the part of a youngster to bring up the discussion of something which naturally embarrasses him. That heroism alone is reason enough to inspire us with respect for even the most sinful, and with affection for even the most far-strayed, lamb.

THE ANSWER

When the youngster has explained his or her problem or stated his or her case, if it is an answer that he expects, the shrewd policy is to make him give that answer himself.

The experienced director handles the problem with a question. He throws the whole thing back to the youngster: "Well what do you think is the answer?"; or "What would be your advice if a friend brought that problem to you?"; or

"Before I give you an answer, I'd like to know how you feel about the whole thing. What would be your solution?"

It's surprising in how many cases the youngster will give exactly the right answer, and then all that the guide has to do is to confirm it. If the youngster's solution is correct, he is well along the right path, and the guide can give him an approving pat on the back and send him blithely on his way. Young people have a well-developed sense of right and wrong. Instinctively or under guidance of God or their conscience they stumble onto the right answers. Alone they distrust their solutions. When they present a solution in answer to your leading question and you confirm their decision, they are delighted. What's more, they are more likely to remember a solution that they have arrived at through your questioning than they are likely to remember a categoric answer that you hurl at their heads.

The best teacher is the one who draws out. Anyone can pour in. The commonplace magician's assistant puts the rabbits into the hat; the magician pulls the rabbits out of the hat. The more the child or the growing young person is helped to form his own opinions and shape his own judgments, the more self-reliant and competent he will become.

But let's say that the young person does not know the answer. He has come to you for guidance and counsel, and you must give him what he seeks. Here is a problem that needs a solution. Here is a question that demands a reply. He wants direction about a course of action that is, he feels, outside the realm and range of his own experience. So the answer is up to the guide.

If it is at all possible, the experienced guide gives the complete answer first in as brief a form as possible. If the answer can be a monosyllable, he should say: "The answer is yes," or "The answer is no"; "You were right," or "This time you are mistaken."

That brief categoric answer settles in a general way the problem that has been troubling the youngster, and he settles back, contented. He was right, and he sighs in relief. He was wrong, but at least he knows the worst, which, he tells you, or himself, he suspected all the while.

When the case requires a solution, a statement of something to be done, this too should if possible be given at once and with definiteness.

"In a case like this I believe your best course is to drop the young man"; or "Certainly you are justified in going ahead"; or "I feel that with your talents you can safely follow the career you have in mind."

The solution is what young people really want. They want to see that solution as rapidly and as completely as possible. The reasons for the particular solution or the decision are important, but they are secondary to the decision itself. Hence, though art and good literature might suggest that you give all the reasons first and then lead up to the solution or the decision as a climax, good psychology demands that you completely reverse the order. And so does good journalism: Put all the important details in the first paragraph; the less important ones can come later.

But these less important details should be given. Sometimes the young person says, "Thanks; that's fine. Never mind the reasons; all I wanted was the answer." More often, completely relaxed by a favorable decision or perhaps a little crushed by an unfavorable decision—but relieved nevertheless—he will sit back and wait to learn why his counselor has arrived at this decision. The wise counselor then gives him the reasons.

"I arrived at that decision for the following reasons: First . . . Second . . . Third . . . "

In conclusion the counselor should restate his decision, briefly summarize his reasons, and in a neat little logical bundle present the whole case to the young person.

Not always however can the counselor give an immediate decision. In that case he is wise to allow a brief interlude.

"That's an interesting and rather unusual problem, and we've got some points to thrash out before I can give you an exact answer. Sit back and have a cigarette . . . or there are some chocolates over there; help yourself. Make yourself comfortable, and let's see how we can get this thing straightened out."

The young person, who during the course of his confidence has probably edged forward toward the very limits of the chair, sits back. The cigarette or the chocolates serve as a pleasant distraction. The counselor gathers his resources together and turns the problem over in his mind.

Then he asks the questions that must be answered before he can see light and give the solution.

"Now you won't, I hope, mind my asking a few questions about some points that are not quite clear to me, will you? First of all, how does it happen . . ."

And out of the confusion that may have accompanied even the well-rehearsed tale, the counselor assembles into order and clarity all the data which he needs for the solution of the problem.

RETORTS

The neat little logical bundle which contains the solution is now with the young person. But he may not be satisfied. His inclination may be to appeal against his counselor's decision. There are angles on the case, he feels, that the counselor has not understood. Sometimes the youngster feels that his counselor has actually been too easy on him, and his protest is a protest against being let off without sterner treatment. "Give me a bigger penance, father," a youngster will occasionally say; "I rate something bigger than ten Our Father's and ten Hail Mary's." Or in all humility he will say: "You're nice to make me feel that I'm not too hopeless, but you're being too easy on me." Young people are often very hard on themselves and demand that we too be stern with them.

So time must be allowed for questions and objections. Counter-arguments should be definitely encouraged. If the young person has a case that he feels he can make, this is certainly the time for him to make it. It would be too bad if after all this embarrassment and effort on his part the case were not settled as completely and definitely as possible. And the case will not be settled until he has dragged into the light the viewpoints and problems that surround it.

The wise director, man or woman, likes a good honest fight for a cause, even if it is a cause of which he does not approve. And the director may be sure too that the youngster who honestly and sincerely insists on and develops a healthy opposition will, with that same honesty and sincerity, accept and carry through the ultimate solution. I myself am a little suspicious of the young person who too readily accepts my decision. His acquiescence may be a subtle youthful flattery. A good battle of arguments is a much more healthy sign of an honest and alert mind than is a too-ready acceptance of a decision. When a boy or a girl will stand up to you and state his position and force you to take it from him point by point, he is telling you that he really likes you and has confidence in you.

The questions which youngsters ask are on occasion so silly and stupid, the problems presented for our grave consideration so utterly unimportant, that inside us there bubbles up a spring of laughter. We feel that the situation calls for a good hoot. But we control our inclination to mirth.

But whether we control our mirth easily or with difficulty, we are fools if we don't control it. No young person ever thinks that a question seriously presented deserves anything but serious consideration. A laugh is never an answer; mirth is never an argument.

And this is a good point at which to discuss the whole question of humor in dealing with youngsters.

Young people like to laugh. A public address or an informal talk to a young audience, when that address or talk is shot through with humor, goes right to their hearts. But then, isn't it true of us all?

There is this difference, though, between young people and us oldsters: Humor, of all human reactions, develops latest in life. Hence youngsters are quick to suspect that laughter is not *for* them but *at* them.

Woe to that guide of youth who laughs at any of the young people who come to him in trust. So, be it ever so silly or ever so light, the wise counselor stifles any slightest inclination to toss a question or a problem aside with a joke and a laugh; he gives to it his most serious attention.

In general no humor should ever be directed at young persons. In the first place, humor puts them hopelessly at the mercy of their elders. They dare not snap back with a bright remark. They hesitate about laughing at their grave and revered seniors. They are in the position of an inferior who has to take the joke made at his expense and pretend to like it. They are forbidden to strike back.

A joke may often relieve the tension of a serious conference when the young person is nervous and on the verge of exploding. The joke must, however, be impersonal. It must not be directed at him, nor should it be applicable to him. I've known children and adolescents and young men and young women in college who have boiled over at the facetious "cracks" of some priest or nun. "He's sarcastic," they say, and with that phrase they damn him to the worst ranks of youth's enemies.

If a girl is notably pretty, one may josh her mildly about her looking like an ugly duckling. "How did the family ever get such an ugly duckling in the flock?" clearly means that everyone knows that the girl is good looking; she enjoys being twitted about a characteristic that she knows she does not possess.

"Well I notice you missed three forward passes," one may say to the young football end who snared four and scored two touchdowns in the weekend game.

But to suggest to a stout girl that her stoutness is funny, or to the young orator who broke down or stammered in his speech that his failure was a joke—to twit a young person about anything that he has done badly — is invariably fatal. But again we are not unlike these youngsters; such tactics would be more or less fatal with all of us. We don't mind being joshed about things we did not do. We enjoy being kidded only about our good points or hearing our excellences talked about in a joke.

All this is merely prelude to the patent fact that under no circumstances should a counselor or a guide belittle or ridicule the young person who presents a difficulty.

"Well I should think that a supposedly smart person like you would have more sense than to . . ." is precisely the formula not to use in dealing with young people. "You blundered into that like a cow, didn't you?"; "Are all the children in your family as dumb as you are?"; "Mickey Mouse would have had more sense than to do a thing like that." Such comments are terrible.

Reverence and respect are never more necessary than in your dealings with young people. Young people have to be very, very sure that you love them and are heart and soul devoted to them before they will receive with good grace even your mild shafts of satire and humor.

KEEPING THE CONFIDENCE

The Church, wise old mother that she is, early discovered that confession would be an intolerable burden were the penitent not guaranteed the most absolute secrecy. So she placed upon the father confessor an obligation of secrecy that is unique among all human relationships. If keeping the seal of confession meant being martyred, then the priest must march with sealed mouth to the fire or to the gibbet. No reason was strong enough to justify the betrayal of a secret whispered in the darkness of the confessional to the man who for the moment was taking Christ's place.

I recommend that all guides of youth make a prayerful meditation on that attitude of the Church. The secret of the confessional is the most absolute secret in the world. But the training and the habit which make priests regard confessional confidences as confidences to be buried in them and with them is the training and the habit that should mark every man or woman who has to deal with the confidences of young people.

Nothing else so completely destroys youngsters' trust in elders as does the betrayal of a confidence. And perhaps because their respect for the seal of confession is so terribly exact, priests and religious have not always felt bound to keep secret what is told to them outside the confessional.

What children or young persons tell to a priest, to a religious, or to a lay guide of youth is a secret that no power on earth should make him violate. I mean all this very seriously. There have been priests who have violated confidences. There have been nuns who in sudden joy have mentioned things told them in confidence. Lay men and lay women have let slip things told them by youngsters. And the youngsters have turned away and have never wholly trusted an older person again. Once more, can we blame these youngsters?

It has been known that religious superiors, again notably in women's communities, have felt that youngsters' confidences given to other religious of the community should be passed on to them. Why, in heaven's name? How can they justify their assumed right to demand that a priest or a brother or a sister who has been trusted with some problem or secret by a boy or a girl should impart that secret to the superior? The young person chose that religious because he trusted him. Now the superior demands that the young person's private affairs be transferred. Again I ask: Why?

The plain fact is that such a demand is a complete overstepping of bounds. A secret is a secret, and a confidence is a confidence. The fact that a person is the superior of a religious community does not mean that the members of that community must pass on to the superior, in addition to their own soul's secrets, the secrets intrusted to them by others. Superiors who actually demand such a thing are asking of their religious dependents a betrayal of confidence and a violation of trust.

There are cases where it is necessary to consult someone else. A young person puts up to a counselor a problem that the counselor does not feel able to handle. The guide is quite within his rights when he says to the confider: "I am not very certain about the answer to your problem; I shall have to consult someone else." But there should immediately be added this assurance: "I guarantee of course that I shall not betray the person who consulted me."

Then the counselor may approach the superior. But the superior is not justified in demanding the name of the person involved. The guide may however prefer to consult someone else whose opinion he values. He is by no means obliged to take his problems to the superior.

When a child or a young person gives a confidence, he does it without compulsion; he does it of his own free choice. This free action of his bars the confidant from retailing the matter to the superior.

Superiors have absolutely no right to demand that they be made the depository of the confidences given to the members of their community. No right whatsoever. They may be doing serious harm to their organization and be violating their own consciences and the consciences of others if they make and are successful in enforcing any such demands. They will be extremely wise if they prayerfully examine themselves on this point.

It is possible to imagine a situation in which, let's say, the young person brings to the confidant a tale of evildoing that involves others. Let us say that it is a growing practice, for example, that is doing real harm to a school. Others are being dragged into sin. The morale of the school is being undermined.

Sabetti-Barrett maintains regarding this: "A just cause for manifesting a secret, even a *secretum commissum*, is that harm is to come . . . to innocent individuals, or to the owner of the secret, or to the one to whom it is confided."

Even in such a case it may be a mistake to take the secret immediately to the superior. If such conduct on the part of the guide were to endanger the confidences or the trust of many young persons, the obligation to tell the secret would not exist. The prudent counselor will realize that a young person whose good will was such that it led him to reveal a perilous condition or situation will in all likelihood have the good will to permit the secret to be told to or used by the proper person or persons. The counselor's efforts should be directed toward getting the young person who confided the secret to grant him leave to act on it.

In all cases it is essential that the confidence of young people in their elders should not be destroyed. The choice of what course to take is something that rests on the wise judgment of the counselor. And a secret is a secret and should be treated with the most exact respect.

Most betrayals of confidence are accidental. A young woman tells her favorite nun friend that she is going to enter the novitiate. The news is so exhilarating that the nun cannot keep it to herself. So she tells her best friend. Her best friend sends the news to one of last year's graduates, who is now in the novitiate. The new novice tells the news to a fellow novice, who writes back to her best friend on the faculty. Within a week the poor prospective nun, who really hoped to have a few undisturbed weeks for a last mild fling, finds that she is branded. "Oh, I hear you are going to the convent." "Isn't it strange for a girl that's going to the convent to be going to the movies so often?" "I'd ask you to the party, but I don't suppose you want to go—now that you're headed for the convent."

And the young woman feels that she has been betrayed.

Perhaps she enters upon her new life with an ingrained suspicion of anyone who seems to encourage her confidences.

There is the little trick of revealing confidences without actually telling anything—a childish trick. A young person gives an older person a confidence; in a crowd later on there is discussion of a subject connected with the general subject of the confidence; the confidant looks at the confider in a knowing way and says, "We understand that sort of thing, don't we?" Of course there has been no betrayal of confidence. But the young person is startled and suspicious. Did the others in the group suspect anything? Did they see through the hint? And why did the older person have to make that remark anyhow?

Or when the confiding person is in the group or close by, the older person tells of "a case that I knew once in which . . ." He gives what is practically the story of the confider. Wise professors of moral theology instruct young confessors never to say, "Once on a time I heard in confession . . ." even when there is the certainty that the person connected with the story is miles away or even dead. Perhaps there is among the listeners a person who has told a similar story in confession, and the suspicion of that person is, "He's talking about me." Or if the story is in no way like his own case, he may jump to this conclusion: "If I talk to him, he may use my case as an example some day. I shouldn't like that."

The simple rule about confidences is that they should be buried in our hearts; and unless we are released by the person who gives them to us, they should be buried with us. If we need help for the solution of a problem brought to us, we ask permission to get that help, and we promise to conceal the identity of the young person most carefully. Neither our superior nor our closest friend should share the secrets which young people entrust to us. The secrets belong to the confiders. Those secrets were lent to us, not given to us. We are no more than trustees. We cannot use those secrets freely as our own. Telling them to others is a misdeed, a kind of theft. It is the misappropriation of someone else's property.

The man or the woman whose heart is a sealed box in

which secrets are placed so securely that no slightest gesture can ever betray them is the man or the woman who wins and keeps the confidence and trust of young people. The man or the woman whose mind is like a sieve will soon find himself or herself with no secrets to pour out. Young people recognize those who are close-mouthed. They hate and regard with contempt a babbler, man or woman. And babblers, regrettable to note, are to be found among men and women.

Confidences on Anything

A guide of youth should be ready to accept confidences and give counsel on any question or problem. Young people expect this readiness and preparedness on the part of elders. That is the compliment that youth pays to maturity and to age, the compliment of expecting from counselors and guides a universal wisdom and a mastery of all the problems that arise in the life of man.

And the guide that is fit to be entrusted with the care of youth comes after a time fairly well toward meeting youth's expectations. The young person may come in and talk about anything that interests or disturbs him. And the older person listens with an open mind. Never does the counselor by gesture or by word imply or say: "I don't think that is a subject you ought to discuss with me." If the child or the growing person, boy or girl, thinks that his interest or problem is a subject for discussion, as far as the counselor is concerned it is a subject to be discussed.

With rather surprising frequency you will run across cases where girls will tell you how their mothers caught them up sharply when they broached the subject of sex or a difficulty connected with sex. I have alternately grinned and gnashed my teeth over the story that was told me by an elderly lady. When she was a little girl, she went to her mother and in all simplicity and with a desire for knowledge (a legitimate desire, after all) asked how babies came into the world.

The mother turned upon her an indignant eye.

"Why!" she cried, drawing back in horror. "You talk like a woman of the streets."

The child felt as if she had been struck. Another problem was thrust into her already muddled mind. What in the world was a woman of the streets? And how did a woman of the streets talk? So the youngster went through adolescence with the feeling that anything connected with the origin of babies must be something quite vile.

A college woman told me of an incident that had occurred in a class of child psychology, which she was attending. The sister in charge of the class turned the pages of the first few chapters with a finger that gingerly avoided contamination with the printed page. "These first few chapters are so unpleasant that we will skip them," she said. So after class the girls rushed from the room, sat down in the corridor, and devoured those first chapters. Those chapters dealt with prenatal and natal data and care.

Again the rule is simple: If the young person thinks that the subject is important enough to warrant his asking about it, the guide of youth should regard it in the same light and should be willing to handle it. He can with justice draw away only when he does not know the answer or the solution. In that case he should admit his ignorance and not crouch behind assumed modesty or shyness.

The prospective guide is rather floored by the realization that he will be expected to handle any question that a young person may bring up. It is true that again and again his questioners will get him into depths well over his head. But in general the type of questions that he will be asked and problems that will be proposed to him will have a marked sameness. I have noted that difficulties and problems are pretty much the same—in various parts of the country and among quite divergent groups.

There are problems that are common to people of a certain age. There are problems that confront most girls; problems that confront most boys. The gamut of questions is not a long one. For quite a time I conducted a question box in connection with each of the retreats I gave. The content was pretty stereotyped. Only occasionally did I get a question that was completely out of the ordinary. Usually the questions were not too stiff or too perplexing. In fact the run of the mill was sufficiently consistent to make the unusual question almost a delight.

The same is true of the questions which young people ask when they come to you for help.

So although the guide of youth must keep himself very alert, must read and observe, must keep abreast of current questions, and must have in his "recognizing" vocabulary the names and to some extent the contemporary slang with which young people are familiar, his interest in young people will make his position not too difficult. Youngsters educate their elders who are interested in them almost as much as the elders educate the youngsters. If a man or a woman keeps his ears and his mind open, he picks up much of the patter and a great deal of the thought current among young people.

Anyway it is the readiness to meet any of their problems that is essential. Wisdom and knowledge advance with experience. Certainly any man or woman who deals with young people has a splendid excuse for keeping on his toes. Mere association with young minds and young interests is excellent preparation for the meeting of the problems they will present.

So briefly: Young people have a right to expect from their guides guidance in anything that is of concern to them. The counselors — and that includes all priests, religious teachers, and lay men and lay women who work with youth— must train themselves to handle all the routine problems and difficulties of youth. Nothing whatsoever is outside the right of youth to bring to the attention of their counselors. Nothing need be outside the range of a counselor's consideration.

A large order, but not nearly so difficult as it may seem at first sight.

PROBLEMS OF FAITH

Rare indeed is the intelligent young person who does not sooner or later run into troublesome problems of faith. Those problems may arise from his reading, from his associates— Catholic as well as non-Catholic — from his own hesitant musing, from the current questions that often involve moral or religious issues. I should be inclined to fear that the boy or the girl who sails along smoothly without problems connected with faith is an unthinking young animal whose highest interest is football or a date for Friday night's dance. God may protect some great saints from problems of faith. But in the ordinary young person such problems are signs that he has started to do some thinking.

A counselor soon finds one consoling fact: a problem of faith that is stated is usually a problem that is half solved. When the young person has pulled the troublesome difficulty out of his mind and has laid it before the calm mind of a priest or a religious, he is somewhat like the sufferer who manages to pull the hard splinter out of his foot. There will still be pain, but the wound is well along the road to recovery.

So, far from discouraging young people from presenting the doubts that tempt them, we should encourage the discussion of such difficulties. For the danger really lies in the situation of the young man or the young woman who does not present such doubts. If doubts are locked in the secret heart and conned over and over again with half knowledge or no knowledge at all, they become toxic. A doubt aired is a doubt almost dissolved. The doubt that is struggled with in secret, that is rolled over and over in the mind and scanned with untrained and troubled eyes is the doubt that poisons.

So be glad when the youngster presents his doubts about faith. And encourage him to present those doubts as strongly and as vigorously as he can. If he makes the best possible case for them, presents them with what he thinks to be crushing force, gets the whole thing once and for all out of his system, a great step has been taken toward the cure of that youngster's soul. The doubt is already more than half solved.

Naturally, with the wide range of subjects covered by faith, doubts may take innumerable forms. In young people however the types are often fairly consistent. The same doubts are to be found in most young people.

Free will is far up on the list of youngsters' doubts. It is almost amusing that at a time of life when they are least bothered with constraint and obligation they should be most worried about whether or not they are free. One ancient fallacy always used in argument against free will always floors them. Every young person has heard it; every young person has stumbled over it in a sweat of sharp apprehension; every youngster looks at it with the feeling: "Well that certainly knocks my life into a cocked hat."

You will recognize the difficulty at once:

"If God knows whether or not your soul is going to be saved, what is the sense in trying to be good? If He sees that you are going to be saved, you are going to be saved —and that's all there is to it. If He sees that you are going to hell, you are going to hell—and all the worrying in the world won't save you."

I remember hearing this problem discussed most inexpertly by some older people who were sitting on the veranda of a summer hotel. The thing struck my soul and came as close to spoiling my carefree summer as anything could. There was no one there to tell me that what God really foresees is whether or not I will freely do those things which take a man to heaven or to hell.

The problem of evil is common in most youthful doubts. Usually the problem is the result of a shock. Young people are shocked at the discrepancy between theory and practice in people around them, in historical characters, in churchmen—ancient and modern. Why do people sin?

Evolution and the popular science connected with it is a problem that troubles the modern young man and young woman. How far may they accept it? Does it, as the popular attacks on faith insist, destroy the whole idea of original sin? Did we have first parents? What about the Garden of Eden? Was the sin of our first parents a sin of impurity? What about Noah and the Ark? What about the six days of creation? What about Jonah and the whale?

Biblical difficulties, in the parodied form which is usually used by the nonbeliever, get into their minds and bother them. Brilliant cynicism or a basic attack on things they thought essential seems at first to blind the youngsters.

A good many of their problems result from their reading of newspapers and magazines. Isn't divorce a very sensible thing? Aren't marriage laws too strict? How could the world get along without birth control? A young Catholic once put that question to me in this way: "The Church is clearly wrong in her atttiude toward birth control. And if she is wrong on so essential a thing, I don't see how it is possible to believe in her infallibility." The handling of that difficulty did not touch a matter of faith; it necessitated showing the terrible harm that birth control is doing to the human race and to our nation.

Along the same line: What, if anything, has the Church done for labor? Isn't the Church the supporter of tyrants and despots? Democracy is usually pagan, isn't it?

Occasionally one meets boys and girls who have had no Catholic training at all—they are commonly found in the freshman classes of our colleges, to which they have come from public high schools—and they are all muddled about truth and goodness. Is there really such a thing as truth? Isn't it a fact that what is true today is likely to be false tomorrow? And how can anyone talk about objective standards of goodness and morality when convention and climate and the shifting of fashion and human necessities are such important factors?

These are just a few of the typical problems that youth faces when faith is first brought to an accounting. The guide of youth, notably the priest or the religious teacher, would do well to have clear, logical, graphic answers to all these difficulties. He will be called on to use those answers more times than he can count.

APPROACHING THE ANSWER

Time was when in Catholic countries the crushing argument against any doubt was: "The Church says so, and it is so." During the time of the English persecution, for example, when Ireland was fighting for the faith, that argument was tremendously powerful. To deny the faith was for an Irishman the same thing as to turn traitor to his country.

The Church and Ireland went hand in hand. Betray one, and you betrayed both. Question the beauty and the truth and the goodness of one, and you hurled doubt into the face of the other. Our clergy of Irish extraction sometimes recall those happy days and think that in this very different day and extremely different country the old argument is still as powerful as it once was. They crush all difficulties with a simple "The Church teaches that, so the matter is closed."

Now a little thought will make the counselor realize that such an answer is today far from adequate. Too much is presupposed in that answer. The young person is treated as if he had a pretty broad and convincing knowledge. I'll grant that *if* it has been proved to him that the Church is Christ's voice in the world; *if* he has studied the eternal rightness of the Church, as history illustrates it; *if* he has gone into the whole question of the teaching function of the Church, which is guided and inspired by the living presence of the Holy Spirit; *if* he knows that from Peter to Pius the Church, and only the Church, has an unbroken record of sticking to its decisions and of not withdrawing from any of them—*if* he knows all this, the argument "The Church says so" is a great and overwhelming one.

But does he know all this?

The modern child lives in an atomsphere that is intellectually hostile to the Church. Every decision that the Church makes or has made is today questioned or ridiculed or denied. The child's country is overwhelmingly non-Catholic. What he reads is Protestant or pagan. His mind is by no means adjusted to any easy formula by which patriotism and faith are connected by an = sign. He hears the Church constantly called into question and her rightness savagely attacked.

To meet his problem or difficulty against faith then with

"The Church says so" will in the vast majority of cases seem to him a simple begging of the question.

"That's just the point," he says; "the Church says so. Well I still don't see it. What's more, I don't see why the Church says so. And if she says so, how do I know she's not wrong?"

When our counselors and guides and teachers of religion and priests in the pulpit have taken time to prove all the preambles to faith and the teaching function of the Church and its proved infallibility, then they can handle all difficulties with the formula "The Church says so." But only then.

I doubt that all these proofs have been presented to the average young person.

Meanwhile that pat reference to the authority of the Church, that answer slapped in the faces of inquiring young people in priests' parlors and in classrooms does no more than produce sulkiness, resentfulness, and a return to doubts. I've met scores of young people who have been treated in this way and who have reacted most unfavorably.

The sincere young fellow who happens by bad luck to be in a non-Catholic school drops in on the priest to get some help. He has a real difficulty; the difficulty isn't making him very happy; in fact he is hoping and praying for a solution.

The priest is busy, and he handles the whole matter rather rapidly.

"So you're in a non-Catholic school, are you? Well what do you expect except doubts against your faith? That difficulty is a silly and a stupid one. I'm ashamed that a Catholic boy has it. The Church teaches the exact opposite; and for any young man with real faith, that's answer enough.

Now go back and say your prayers and ask God to give you faith—and a little common sense."

The boy goes back, but his reaction is probably this:

"Oh! so the old fourflusher didn't know the answer, eh? Thought he could wiggle out of it by hiding behind 'the Church says so.' He was stumped all right. I'm to meet difficulties against the faith by praying myself into a 'will to believe,' am I? I'm to hypnotize myself back into the Church. Well I'm sorry. I'd certainly like to be a Catholic. But if that's the way the Church handles honest problems, excuse me."

And on a shelf of the priest's library is a book or a pamphlet which someone has written about that particular difficulty because he thought it deserved honest consideration and an intelligent answer.

You can't hurl the Church at a doubting head, unless that head knows a great deal about the Church. "The Church says so" leaves the modern young doubter cold. Too bad perhaps; but we may as well face facts. Perhaps the fault is largely with us oldsters who have failed to make the Church attractive and convincing to youthful eyes.

Handling a Problem Against Faith

In most cases the wrong way to start handling a problem of faith is to start handling the problem of faith.

Faith is not merely a matter of the intellect. Nor is doubt simply a matter of the mind. Often enough doubt is mixed up with emotions of the most complex sort. The young husband who comes arguing furiously in favor of birth-control legislation is probably emotionally disturbed because of his desire to practice birth control. The young college woman who pleads for the cause of man's evolution from the beast may have heard that doctrine from a very fascinating young instructor who appealed to her somewhat after the fashion of an outstanding motion-picture hero. It has sometimes been noted that young people lose their faith in non-Catholic colleges, not because of the intellectual arguments in the classroom, but because of the charm and good manners and fine breeding and intelligence of those whom they meet and with whom they associate in the college.

To smash right into the argument and to batter the problem to pieces with strong and lusty logical blows is often the most ineffective approach.

It is well to size up the objector, to study him well, to put him completely at his ease, to make him like you before you tackle the question itself.

I have found that a good approach is to pay a gesture of respect to the problem: "Yes. I've heard that problem before. It really stumps many people. I'm not surprised that you are puzzled. May I ask where you heard it or read it?"

The incipient doubter is thus thrown from the problem to the things that lie around the problem. He read it in H. G. Wells or in the Sunday supplement. An attractive young chap with whom he camped last summer brought up the subject. A crowd of his friends were discussing the question the other night, and he thought the Catholic in the crowd made rather a fool of himself.

The necessity for talking around the problem has put the young person at his ease and has given you a deal of valuable data that show you whether his difficulty is really intellectual or whether it is tied in with powerful and persuasive emotional reactions. He has for the time being dropped what was perhaps a belligerently aggressive attitude and has slipped into straight narrative. Your next step is comparatively easy.

That next step may be a calm discussion of the sort of person who runs into that particular difficulty or doubt.

"That is a doubt that comes to a great many young people who are between the ages of, let's say, sixteen and twenty-six. . . . Yes. I've found that college people bring that up fairly often. . . . It's a problem that young married people often meet. . . . It's surprising how many boys . . . or girls . . . or high-school students have worried about that."

If you happen to know the author who suggested the doubt (if the difficulty came from a book), you may even mention or imply that you know him and his writings. But if you don't know the author, don't pretend that you do. It takes a brilliant faker to discuss an author he knows nothing about with a person who has read that author— however young that reader may be. Often it is possible, if one knows the particular author well, to show precisely why the writer brought up such and such a difficulty or held such and such a view. Fatal is the policy of lacing into the author and damning him for an ignoramus. He probably isn't an ignoramus. And even if he were, he still would not seem so in the eyes of the youthful disciple who has just quoted him.

I should make an exception where the obviously insincere and dishonest author is concerned. The Haldeman-Julius Press has a serpentine way of getting its anti-God, anti-Catholic, antimoral books into the hands of young people. I have found the Little Blue Books in surprising places. That gang of authors and printers deserve neither consideration nor courtesy. They are the logical successors of the bigoted, lying, anti-Catholic paper from which they spawned. Many of those authors are like the notorious Joseph McCabe, who in his apostate wrath writes lies with the fluency of a syndicated versifier writing bad poetry. If you are sure that the author or publisher is dishonest and a liar, it is just as well to smash him and try to break his hold on your youthful charge.

Most reputable authors however should be treated with respectful consideration. They write well. Most of them write with much sincerity. We do not prejudice the case in our favor when we slash out at writers whom the young inquirer may sincerely respect.

In the same way, if the inquirer seems to be intelligent, it may be wise to explain why at certain periods of life certain difficulties occur. The difficulty against free will bangs hard into a young person because he has not had the lifelong experience of exercising that free will; and he has never seen the malicious use of free will thwarting good and promoting evil. Biblical difficulties come to him because in grammar school he was given the literal story; now he sees the flashy difficulties against the background of the literal explanation; he knows nothing of the extremely difficult sciences which fumble and stumble about amid the records and ruins of the past; he has not learned to realize that a flat statement like "Moses couldn't write" proves nothing, or that highly colored reconstructions of manuscripts and mammals and monuments are often one part fact and ninety-nine parts fiction.

Kindly, but with candor, it may be possible to show the young person why at this period of his life that difficulty or this one occurs. But the greatest care must be exercised not to hurt his feelings or wound his youthful sensibilities. No argument is convincing to a person on whose feet you have just trod heavily.

If a man or a woman can do it tactfully, he can say—if this be true—"That's really interesting. When I was about your age, I had that precise difficulty." He can even go on to explain: "I remember very well how it came about. A crowd of us at camp were talking . . ." or "I was reading one of Ibsen's plays . . ." or "I picked up a popular-science book. . ." The authentication of detail is impressive. Youth is drawn to a person who admits to having shared his own somewhat annoying or troubling experience.

THE BEAUTY OF IT

I feel that long before one comes to logical argument with the young person there are preliminary steps that can gracefully and effectively be taken. Let's say for example that the problem concerns a Catholic doctrine. We can of course plunge right into the proofs. We can demonstrate the truth of the doctrine convincingly.

We can however take a more appealing course of action:

"That's really a very interesting doctrine. Have you ever stopped to realize how beautiful it is?

Beautiful. That's a new concept thrown into the case. What's more, it is an extremely appealing concept. Ten to one the young person has never thought of his religion as being beautiful. He has probably been told only that his religion is true and that he had better follow it—or else. Beauty has a quick appeal. And your young charge has probably never thought of the possibilities of the beauty of the doctrine.

It is quite the easiest thing in the world to show the beauty of Catholic doctrine. Free will is certainly marvelously beautiful by comparison with any doctrine of slave will or brute necessity. The fact that God wants to remain in the world in the Blessed Sacrament is beautiful. The whole theory of grace, our sharing of the divine life, is, even taken just as a theory, remarkably noble and inspiring. The Fatherhood of God; the Motherhood of Mary; the beautiful security one finds in following an infallible teacher and not a blundering, hesitating one; the way in which the sacraments supply our needs at every stage of life; the fact of an eternal reward—all these things are exquisite. It is true that the parodies on religion are notably ugly—as ugly as a Puritan church or as the dour face of a Calvinist minister. But we can take the doctrine which the young person finds difficult and show him that, difficult or not, it is a marvelously beautiful doctrine. And one does not mind accepting a difficult thing if it is a beautiful thing.

There is another modern approach that can be made. It is possible to show the young person that most of the Catholic doctrines, even if they were not true, are exactly in accord with the desires of modern man. If most modern religions run pantheistic, we have in the Mystical Body the real unity with God which, while it gives us divine life, still destroys nothing of our individuality.

The desire for God-with-us, which is expressed even in pagan art and literature, ancient and modern, is fulfilled for us by Christ of the tabernacle and by the indwelling of the Holy Ghost. The human solidarity of communism is a poor parody on the Christian solidarity in Christ. Women today are being lifted to new opportunities, but they still have a long way to go before they attain to a dignity like that of the Mother of God. And the list of Catholic doctrines, which are extremely modern in concept, extremely appealing in their approach to human instincts and human desires, is endless.

Beauty and human appeal are more powerful arguments than are syllogisms. Beauty and human appeal reach both the mind and the heart. The syllogism batters at the mind, when perhaps it is the heart which is troubled and rebellious.

Another argument which has remarkable power is the surprise argument. A great many young people cling to the ancient statement *"Credo, quia impossibile,"* "I believe, because the thing is manifestly impossible." It strikes them quite unexpectedly then to be shown that the argument for a certain doctrine is really extremely reasonable, that the whole doctrine in fact appeals to right reason.

A young person comes to you; he is all in a lather because someone has just shown him that he is merely an animal. He does not want to be an animal; but be believes that when the Church says he is not a mere animal, the Church is wrong.

The approach to this difficulty is this: The counselor admits quite readily that there is in our nature a strong element of the animal. For that matter he proves that man is an interesting and complex synthesis of the animal, the vegetable, and the mineral kingdoms. It is quite right that man should be such a synthesis; the lord of the universe should have in him something of all the elements of the universe.

But the counter-argument continues. The fact that the young person does not want to be a mere animal is significant. Evidently he has desires that are not animalistic. More than that; it is a notable thing that the more human a man becomes, the less animal he remains. A poet is not like a bee; a sculptor shows few signs of being a monkey. A hero or an ascetic or a martyr or a saint is honored simply because something in him has triumphed over the animal characteristics of cowardice, gluttony, instinctive self-preservation, selfishness.

"If you are just an animal, doesn't it seem strange that the grievous way in which one man can insult another is to say that he is bestial or that he acts like a brute or that he is a swine, or a dog, or a wolf? And the insult of insults is that of being called a bitch or of being accused of having any connection with one. Man's reason clearly indicates that that part of him which creates, loves, aspires, that part of him which is heroic and noble, which paints, sings or explores is so unlike the beast that nothing in the animal kingdom so much as suggests it. You have to deny your reason and your own instincts before you can level yourself with the brute kingdom."

The instance is merely typical. A thousand other instances could be presented. It is deft and skillful to show, before one launches into argument, that our stand is a reasonable one, one that is eminently human and humane.

The Arguments

The fact that many non-Catholics feel as we do on a certain question is usually something of a surprise. The widespread acceptance of the Real Presence by churches which are not Catholic is a fact often unknown to young people. So is the fact that in all but the most recent Protestant churches confession is a general practice. The non-Catholic acceptance of immortality, of free will, of the need for some sort of religious supreme court is always impressive. And allies from the ranks of scientists are powerfully effective. The recent swing back toward the belief in the existence of souls and in man's immortality—and this in scientific circles —impresses young people. And quite rightly impresses them.

The counselor should present all this prelude in order to prepare the emotions of the young person for the truth. Forgive me if I seem to be mixing things rather badly. What have emotions to do with truth? The mind, the intellect, cold reason deal with truth. Why drag the emotions into the picture?

Well there are several excellent reasons:

First, the emotions are being violently dragged in against faith. The Church is in a logically unassailable position. She has all the arguments on her side. With the guns of dialetics she can batter down the position of any enemy.

Science has hurt her position not at all. History, as it unfolds its hidden and rediscovered pages, sustains the Church in a gratifying fashion.

But the emotions have been enlisted against the Church: The Church is old-fashioned; the Church is intolerant; the Church is the refuge of the ignorant; the Church is out of touch with the scientific mind.

We present the cold logic of infallibility, and all the while the young person may be boggling with any one of a dozen emotional difficulties: "I don't like such and such a priest. . . . This sister was not kind to me. . . . Why don't Spanish Catholics in America go to church? . . . If the Papal encyclicals are such marvelous guides to right action, how do you account for dishonest Catholic businessmen and crooked Catholic politicians? . . ."

The enemy has dragged the emotions into everything. It has slurred the Church and sneered at her; it has ridiculed her and pointed the finger of scorn at her teachings. It has excited prejudices and bigotry and stirred up doubts that were based largely on fears—the fear that perhaps this time the Church is wrong, the fear that the facts may not agree with the theory, the fear that the past of the Church may be pretty sordid and shadowy.

The enemy has appealed directly to the emotions, no question of that. The desire for food, the desire for liberty, the desire for art, the desire for justice—all these things the enemy has played upon in its attack against the Church. And against this, churchmen have perhaps depended too much on the cold syllogism to answer the hot sneer. Churchmen have tried to parry with logic the enemy's onslaught of laughter. Those who hate the faith try to kill it by appealing to the emotions. And we who love the faith must do likewise—we must appeal to the emotions.

Second, it is important to remember that for one person who thinks there are a thousand others who feel. The early Church, realizing this, made a wise appeal. To a world that had forgotten how to think, a world that had raised Sophistic philosophy, the art of distorting truth, to a position supreme among sciences—to this world the early Church appealed through the things that could be seen and felt and loved. The early Church gave the world the Eucharistic banquet and taught it kindness to the poor; she began the glorious liturgy and gathered the outcasts of society under her chasuble; she showed the world the Son of Man, the most beautiful of all the sons of men, and demonstrated how Christians can love one another. Arguments could come later. The first and greatest appeal was to the eye and to the heart. And that same appeal is one that emotional youth today can understand.

And a third excellent reason for appealing to the emotions, though by no means the last reason, is this: It is important for you to reach the young person's emotions when you are dealing with all matters of faith for the reason that faith is often lost because of misled emotions. The ghosts of those who were slain in the St. Bartholemew-day massacre rise up to peer over the shoulder of the priest who presents the arguments for the holiness of the Church. The sneers that smart writers have cast at hell get between the nun and the girl who are discussing the truth of the Blessed Sacrament. And if sin seems clever and virtue dull, if beauty seems to wrap the world's error close and warm while drab logic and stern argument heavily gird the Church's truth, youth cannot be blamed if it sighs for the cleverness and yearns for the beauty.

That is why the guide who is dealing with youth must emphasize the beauty of Catholic truth. Catholicism is true. Oh, yes. But when you speak to young people it is almost more important that you emphasize the beauty of Catholicism. I have developed the argument at some length in a little booklet called "It's All So Beautiful." But that argument could easily be expanded to fill a tome.

So youth must be shown that Catholic truth answers the desires of man's heart. While it is important that young people know of truth's conformity to the mind of God, they are more impressed by the knowledge that truth answers the desires of men. Truth is not a matter of abstract mathematics. It is regrettable that we have often treated it as if it were. Truth is really a heart-warming thing, the all-satisfying food that God offers to hungry souls. Truth is the answer to man's questioning, the solace for man's weary yearnings.

Skip the logical arguments for a while and show young people that truth lifts up the heart and sets it beating in dance tempo. We have pounded young people with syllogisms. Some day we'll present Catholic truth by singing it to glorious melodies and by marching to it as bands blare forth rousing choruses.

CHRIST'S ATTITUDE

After all it is important for the guide of youth to keep in mind this lovely fact: What we hold about supernatural truths we hold because these truths were given to us by the world's most attractive man. Yes, these truths conform to reason. Certainly they are backed by convincing arguments. Surely they are beautiful and desirable. But, most glorious of all, these truths are the very things which and for which God came from heaven to teach us.

Truths are never more attractive than when they are heard from the lips of the God-Man. The great teacher of youth is and always will be Christ. And we are wisest when we let Christ do His teaching for us. We are most convincing when we let the young people see that it is not we or some brilliant man that thought all these things out, but that they came straight from the Sacred Heart of Him who loved us even unto death.

When we wish to show Christ as a teacher, it is well for us briefly to prepare the ground. I do not believe that we should flash Christ upon the unprepared youngster. We should show briefly:

That Christ is the most modern of men;

That what He taught did not flow out of the heart of a primitive race but came from God and was given to a highly sophisticated people because they could not otherwise be saved;

That even those men who do not admit that Christ was the Messiah admit His greatness as a teacher;

That the world would be gloriously transformed if it accepted His teachings;

That even were He not God, it would still remain true that His wisdom is beyond the wisdom of any man that ever lived.

History or Science

Then against the background of these facts we show youth that Christ taught precisely this truth or that one. If His words are clear (as they are about divorce, for example), His exact words can be used most effectively. If we wish to explain a doctrine, such as the dignity of labor, which Christ illustrated by His own conduct, tell the young person the story of Christ's activities. And if we wish to explain the truth of man's personal redemption, we can give the glowing details of Christ's dying for that truth—and there indeed we give a true picture of romantic heroism.

A young man once said to me:

"I wish I had a nickel for every time I've heard a priest say: 'Of course science is all on the side of faith,' or 'Historical difficulties leave the Church untouched.' But I wish I had a penny for every time a priest made a statement like that without proving it."

It struck me at the time that we are too prone to substitute for our "I say so" the argument "the Church says so." We make sweeping claims about science and history, claims that we do not bother to prove with facts. The proofs are there. Looking them up or rooting them out is a job. It's a snap to throw off a quick "Well everybody knows that modern science today admits . . ." But the cold fact is that everybody does not know what modern science admits, and the young person wants something more tangible than a sweeping gesture.

Broad unsubstantiated gestures weaken our position with the young person. One fact is worth a windmill of gestures. One quotation from a scientist's treatise on immortality, for example, is more convincing than the most eloquent voice that thunders, "Scientists today have thrown in their lot with the immortality of the soul."

If we are tackling a problem of history or of science, we had better handle it, not with oratory and rhetoric, but with history and science. The young person knows when we are substituting words for facts and eloquence for definite data.

So when the difficulty is based on some historical problem or some scientific doubt, the best approach is this:

First, give a brief synoptical answer, stating facts and authorities to establish that answer as true.

Second, recommend or give to the young person a booklet or an article that treats the subject. The chances are that the young person will not read the booklet or the article.

The more profound and the more technically historical or scientific the explanation, the less likely it is that the inquirer will read it. The value of the booklet or the article lies in this: that the young person has had in his hand printed matter that answered his problem. He has seen the printed word in solid paragraphs that march like a formidable army. He may not be able to understand the article; he may not even take time to read it. But the solidity of the text and the marching paragraphs in battle array are convincing. The doubter now sees that a scholar has handled this matter and has answered the difficulty. That is usually answer enough. However if the young person reads the booklet or the article, so much the better.

At Last the Arguments

Now the ground is all prepared for the actual arguments.

"At last," you may say. Yes; at last.

A wise old professor of philosophy gave me some very valuable information when I was a senior in college: "If you have prepared your ground," he said, "you can almost omit your arguments. Arguments are often unnecessary after you have defined your terms, explained your position, given a clear expression of what you hold, and laid down the factors that led you to that stand. You will often find your audience nodding agreement before you even touch on a proof."

All extremely correct. Our mistaken tendency, I repeat, is to plunge into proofs. We rush headlong into arguments. That is all wrong. If we have prepared the ground, if we have explained and made clear our position, if we have shown that this particular truth is beautiful and conforms to reason, if we have brought out the sweet reasonableness of this truth as it fell from the lips of the sweet Christ, argument can take a fourth or a fifth place.

Still the argument must as a rule be given a place. And

this is the time, now that the ground is prepared, for arguments to enter in.

Give the proofs as briefly and as clearly as possible.

You are now safe in resting your case with a conciliated jury.

The Human and the Divine

The Church is a creature composed of body and soul.

The soul of the Church is the abiding, indwelling Holy Spirit.

The body of the Church is made up of the men and women who are members of the Church.

The divine head of the Church is Christ.

The soul of the Church is true and beautiful and eternally right. But the body of the Church includes, regrettably, diseased and spotted members.

Those outside the Church, the very ones who are quite willing ordinarily to make all possible allowances for human frailties and limitations, make little allowance where the Church is concerned. In their minds and in their judgments they make no distinction between bad Popes and infallible Popes; between the sins of a great king and the essential holiness of the Church; between the collapse of the Church in Russia and the unfailing character of the Church Universal. The argument against the Christlike character of the Church is likely to be something like the picture of a medieval bishop who wore armor over his surplice and wielded a battleaxe more zealously than he did a holy-water sprinkler.

In our work as counselors we must early prepare youth to meet the human character that tracks its frequently unpleasant trail across the pages of the Church's divine history. A Catholic professor of history whose opinion I highly value once said that, as he took his class through a particular period of history, he made it a point to inform his students of the contemporaneous evils in the Church.

"They are very likely to read or hear about those evils later on," he explained. "If I don't refer to them in class, the students will be convinced that I dodged the issues or tried to cover them up because I feared that there was no answer. If I face those facts honestly in class and show my students the distinction between the human and the divine, I have warded off later problems."

His was, it seemed to me, a most wholesome prophylaxis.

The human and the divine exist in the Church today as they have from the very first days of the Church. It is wise to cultivate in the young person a clearly distinct vision of these two elements. God is blamed for much too much of what is man's doing. The Church is credited or, more correctly, debited with the stupidities and selfishnesses of churchmen. It is quite understandable that our enemies should make that mistake. It is pitiful if the same mistake is permitted in our own, especially in our youngsters.

On the other hand it may be that we are sometimes too ready to admit the human element in the Church. Certainly great harm was done to the Church in Spain by those exhibitionistic Catholics who, basing their condemnation on the special pleading of the very Spanish calumniators who hated the Church, condemned the Spanish bishops as lazy and incompetent.

We Catholics have not as much *esprit de corps* as we might have. And certainly we are not building up a wholesome attitude in young people when we show too much of the human elements in the Church and too little of the divine elements; or when we praise the divine element to the skies, where they rightly belong, but condemn human elements to the gutter, where they are really quite seldom to be found.

The easy cynicism of certain Catholics—a cynicism which finds so much to commend outside the Church and so little to commend inside the Church, which believes that all non-Catholics are gentlemen and scholars and disinterested heroes and that all Catholic leaders are a trifle on the boorish side, not too intelligent, and notably venal—sometimes slips into our own attitudes.

To admit the human is quite right. To stress the human is a mistake. To find the human where the human does not exist is completely wrong.

The Follow Up

The counselor of youth should have convenient to his hand or carefully indexed in his mind the right book for the right problem. Perhaps more frequently he should have not a book but a booklet. Youth reads as it runs, if it reads at all. And a booklet is about the size of the dose of reading that most young people can swallow.

So to reinforce his handling of the problem, the priest or religious lends the young person a book. For some reason I find the word lending better than the word giving. There is something very personal about going into one's desk or book-case, pulling out a booklet—probably a little thumbed and noticeably used—and saying:

"Now here's a booklet on the subject. I found it interesting. Take it along, and bring it back when you're through with it."

If the young person doesn't bring it back, so much the better.

The personal touch in this lending of the booklet is a charming, persuasive factor. Certainly the gesture is much better than: "Take ten cents to the bookrack and buy such and such a booklet"; or "Here's a book I'll give you. Read it and put it in your own library." A new, clean book is a pretty impersonal sort of thing. Where religion is concerned, a reader is much more impressed by a book that someone else has read so diligently that thumbprints mark the pages than he is by a book in which the pages are still uncut.

The counselor's second meeting with the questioner may be extremely important. Perhaps of his own accord the almost-doubter will bring up the subject of his doubt. If he does, he will probably plunge at once into new difficulties he may have found or points that he still wants cleared up. If he does not do this however the counselor is safe in taking the initiative.

"Have you thought any more about the subject we were talking about?" is an offhand approach that makes easy the reopening of a conversation. The questioner may have been completely satisfied by the counselor's explanation at the first meeting; if so, the matter can safely be dropped. But if he is not satisfied, the counselor now has a chance to restate the case and to clear up the difficulties that were not answered or that were inadequately answered or that were not fully understood at the first meeting.

Problems of faith are necessarily common in the life of the modern young man and young woman. Blessed is that priest or religious to whom young people can bring their problems with the assurance that they will be sympathetically received and respectfully heard. And one cannot resist a scriptural paraphrase: "Woe to you counselors who browbeat or intimidate or sneer at the youngster who has the courage to admit his difficulties against faith!"

"What right has a young whippersnapper like you to have doubts about faith? . . . When you get some brains, I'll talk to you about a difficult subject like that. You must have brains before you can have doubts. What's a youngster like you doing with doubts? . . . So you're going to a public school, are you? Well you can't expect anything else but

doubts when you're constantly in an occasion of sin. . . .
Go home and humble yourself and ask God to forgive you
your pride. The very idea of your rising up and telling God
what's right and what's wrong! . . . You heard me say that
that doubt is nonsense. That's enough. Now stop bothering
yourself and me with such foolishness!"

Imaginary sections of fictitious conversations? I wish to
high heaven that they were imaginary or fictitious. But they
are, regrettably, verbatim greetings and dismissals that young
people have retailed to me—greetings and dismissals that
were accorded young people when, half trembling and
ashamed, they approached a counselor to have their difficulties ironed out and their doubts dissolved. I wonder how the
good Lord regards that shepherd of souls or that counselor
of youth whose lazy mind and easygoing ways leads him to
solve doubt with a sneer and to meet difficulties with bully-
ragging and loud-voiced bluster. Christ was courteous in his
treatment of even the cynical Pilate and the tricky Pharisees.
How much more does an earnest inquirer deserve courtesy!

Many a case of lost faith may be laid at the door of those
counselors of youth who never took the time or the trouble
to find out how youthful doubts and difficulties should be
handled.

THE BOY-AND-GIRL PROBLEM

May I begin this important section on youth guidance
with a few important platitudes?

Most Catholic guides of youth, the priests and the religious, are by vow celibates. That vow is in itself beautiful.
It is a glorious thing that the young man or the young
woman, troubled or distressed or perplexed by temptations
against purity, should know that he or she can take his or her
problems to a man or to a woman who has vowed in special

and solemn agreement to live a life of celibacy and to practice only those things that are pure.

But . . .

(And that little word deserves a line all to itself.)

. . . it is quite wrong to interpret and to judge the conduct of youth in the light of priestly or religious celibacy. And it is absurd to set for young people standards which are the standards only of those chosen souls who have pledged themselves to God and have placed themselves beyond the pale of marriage.

In particular, too many nuns expect nunlike conduct in their girls. Too many nuns demand in girls ideals that are connected with a vow which these girls have not taken. And this attitude is manifestly unfair.

Is this an indictment of priests and religious who take a firm stand on the matter of sin? Certainly not. But it is an indictment of those chaste-by-vow souls who forget that the world is peopled with young men and young women who have not taken solemn vows of chastity. And even if these priests and men and women religious do not forget these things in theory, they certainly forget them in their action toward young people. And pastors too are often as easily misled by their own idealism in this regard as are men and women religious.

There are a few important details for priests and religious to remember. First, God intended boys and girls to be attracted to one another.

That is something that needs frequent repetition in priests' studies and in community recreation rooms. I personally would slightly distrust an adolescent who did not find the members of the opposite sex attractive. I should wonder whether there was something missing in his physical or psychological make-up. I would regard him—and equally her—as not quite normal.

When boys and girls begin to regard one another as unattractive, the end of the world will have come. There will be no more marriage or the giving in marriage, not because men will have become like the angels of God, but because they will have become less than human.

There are boys who at certain periods of their life are not interested in girls. There are girls who at times regard boys as oafs and buffoons. In some cases such attitudes are honest; in some cases they are a pose. But I fear for the future of that adolescent who really and fundamentally dislikes the members of the opposite sex. Such adolescents will not marry; if they do marry, God pity their mates. They are not fit to be priests or religious. And at some time or other some psychological explosion may do untold damage to them and to others.

The second thing to remember is that Marriage is a Great Sacrament. The capitals are less for emphasis than out of deference to St. Paul. Marriage, my dear fellow celibates, is not a substitute for a lost religious vocation. It is not a form of life into which inferior types of men gravitate because they haven't the courage or the ability to be priests or religious. Marriage is a Great Sacrament.

Yet that is certainly not the attitude taken by all counselors of youth. I recall a good priest who gave a most astounding opening conference in his retreat to a group of college girls:

"You are," he told them, "all called to be nuns. Some of you will have the courage and the good sense to answer that call. The less worthy among you, the cowards and the weaklings, will resist that call. For these cowards and weaklings there is only marriage, with its trials and its heavy responsibilities. But if you listen to God, you will all be nuns."

I gave the next retreat to this group of girls, and I was expected to clear up some of the wreckage of that other retreat. For from the moment the priest had made that astounding talk, all the girls, even those who had a vocation to the religious life, simply concluded that he was a fool, and they withdrew into the secret places of their minds. He could not follow them there, and they refused to follow him anywhere.

I have been told by many a young man that priests are interested in him so long as they think he may enter upon the priestly or the religious life. I have been told by many a young girl that nuns are interested in her only so long as they think that she will enter the order.

Far be it from me to condemn any honorable and zealous impulse on our part to have young people live lives like ours, but to carry that impulse to extremes, as I know for a fact so many priests and religious do, is simply to climax the course of wrong reasoning.

Religious life and the priestly life are vocations. But not everyone is fitted for them. There are splendid men and splendid women in the world; sainthood is quite possible in any walk of life. And we must remember that if everyone became a priest or a nun or a brother there would soon be no candidates for the priesthood or for the religious life.

Finally, Marriage is a Great Sacrament. And to look upon it as if it were a poor substitute for a lost religious vocation is absurd and most misleading. No doubt of it; good and holy counselors of youth have not always accorded to the Great Sacrament the respect which Christ and St. Paul accorded to it. Is it surprising then that young people conclude that their guides have only an undisguised contempt for the whole matter of sex relations?

HENCE SOCIAL LIFE

Then into the list of things we celibates must remember goes this important sorites:

God intended boys and girls to be attracted to one another. . . .

If this were not true, the Great Sacrament would have no place in the scheme of the world. . . .

Hence . . .

Well ordered and wholesome social life for youth is natural and right.

And boys and girls quite naturally want social life and have a right to it.

It is possible that in some remote day—the more remote the better—civilization will resume the custom of the giving in marriage, of marriage by parental contract. The day may come when a young man will be promised to a young woman that he has never seen, a promise made on the basis of the admiration of one family for another or the desire of two families to unite an orchard with a near-by meadow. In that day it will probably be the custom to sequester boys and girls, to draw hard and fast lines to separate them. The whole matter of a young man's or a young woman's companion during his or her adult life will be settled by grave elders who will be guided by their prophetic knowledge of the future of the particular young souls.

I hope that day does not come. Perhaps literature is not a fair standard by which to judge, but the literature of those eras and countries in which such customs prevailed seems to indicate that if love did begin with marriage, it was love for someone other than the person whom the young man or the young woman had married.

Young people's unrestricted choice in the matter of their mate may not be too wise. But older people's unrestricted choice in the matter of mates for their children does not seem to have been much wiser. Clearly what is needed is the guiding of young people in their choice.

Young people should be given a certain amount of freedom in the choice of and association with other young people who would make satisfactory mates. And this is what is meant by giving young people a correct, supervised, but very happy social life.

Young people want, and rightly want, to associate with other young people. Association is just another word for social life. Today young people are offered opportunities for that social life under the most unwholesome conditions. We counselors and guides have a clear alternative: Shall we help young people to live their lives correctly? Or shall we leave that work to the enemies of God and of morality? The decision rests with us.

The next point I want to make is a reassuring one:

It is my reasoned conviction, checked by the experience of a large number of priests and religious with whom I have talked, that among decent young people there is far less sin or occasion for sin than shocked rumor seems to indicate. Oh, there is sin, and sin in plenty. The jazz party of the last generation, the easy drinking of the prohibition and post-prohibition eras, the onslaughts which those writers and teachers who have been youth's great betrayers have conducted against sex modesty and sex decency—all these have taken their toll in sin; all these embody precisely what we mean by unwholesome association and unsupervised social life.

What I believe is this: When decent young people, with the normal safeguards thrown around them, dance together, or picnic together, or play games, or meet in one another's homes, or go out in foursomes or in larger groups, sin is by no means a common occurrence. Youth is fundamentally sound; the tendency to look on all of youth's social contacts as occasions of sin is simple nonsense.

A certain type of religious is thrown into a dither if she notices that a young boy and a young girl are interested in each other. If she sees these two running or playing together, she is close to fainting. There have been priests who who have made ridiculous statements such as, "Young people cannot dance together without being in a proximate occasion of sin." And whole systems of education have in certain times and places been built up on the supposition that if a prefect did not stand guard over a student day and night, that student would shoot straight for the goal of sin. As far as I can make out, when that particular kind of prefect has stood guard for a time and was then removed, his prophecy stood a good chance of being fulfilled.

In the boy-girl relationship among decent people there is, let me repeat, far less sin than the scandal shouters would have us believe exists.

COMPETITION FOR YOUTH

The competition for the allegiance of youth is being conducted, as everyone knows, along the lines of social-life activities. The radical groups and the reactionary groups, communists and nazis alike, win youth to their cause largely through recreational programs. The briefest glance at the newspapers' rotogravure sections reveals that. The attack on youth's morals has been directed largely against his leisure and recreational activities. The "new morality," which is of course as old as the first sinner and as moral as Cain's crime, is presented to young people when they are at the theater, or when they are reading the easy-to-scan magazine, or when they are paging through the hot-off-the-press novel.

The party in which there was utterly unwholesome drinking and rankly pagan dancing—the kind of social life that lowered the conventional standards—has spread its taboo to the party in which there is perfectly wholesome dancing and wholesome enjoyment. The boy and the girl who are out on a date are almost automatically marked as a boy and a girl who treat purity as a badly dated superstition and who accept easy promiscuity and casual exchange of affection that border on passion.

Today the Catholic counselor who is fighting for youth must contend with the shrewdest entertainment forces in the world. Playtime is now shot through with temptation. The leisurely mind has within easy reach a thousand incitements to sin and to low standards of decency.

Training the Parents

Wouldn't it be grand if we could settle this whole matter of youth's social life by tossing it right back where it belongs, to the parents?

Wouldn't it be perfect if we could say: "Social life is no problem. Our Catholic homes are the centers of social life"?

Wouldn't it be ideal if, when any suggestion of sex education were brought up, our answer could be: "We don't have to teach our young people about these matters; their parents have handled all that most adequately"?

And wouldn't it be gloriously Catholic and right if mothers and fathers were guiding their own children in all that regards the boy-and-girl relationship?

Wouldn't it?

Oh, wouldn't it!

Perhaps we shall have solved the whole question of the attitude of boys and girls toward one another when we have cleared up the question of the attitude of parents toward their own children. When homes become the centers of social life, when the boy brings home the girl in whom he is interested, when the girl introduces the boy to sympathetic and interested parents, when a boy goes to his father—or rather when a father brings his son to him—to learn all that he needs to know about sex, and when a mother shares the confidences of her daughter to such an extent that the girl's difficulties of adolescence are discussed and cleared up without embarrassment or surprise or even a slight quiver of loathing . . .

Then, no doubt, the millennium for youth will have arrived.

Perhaps I would be wise to conclude this whole booklet at this particular point by saying: "Guides of youth, your first great job is to be guides of the parents of youth." I might at this point urge a course of study for parents. To teach parents how to make the home over which they rule a perfect center of social life for their children would be a great step toward the solution of all of youth's problems.

Maybe we guides and counselors could give back to the parents—to whom it belongs—the whole matter of the guidance of their youngsters in all that concerns social life and the relationship between boys and girls.

But since it is likely that we are long years from the millennium, and since not all Catholic homes are centers of social life, and since parents do not guide their children and in most cases do not even talk to them, and since only very rarely do parents come to us, and since children and young people do come to us, it is we who must go ahead with the problems of youth.

And it will remain our job until a great number of parents begin to do their duty intelligently.

This Matter of Sex

The attraction of a boy to girls is based, as everyone knows, on the incipient or adolescent or developed power of sex.

The realest trouble about sex guidance is simply this: All the wrong people have instructed youth about sex, and all the right people either have been criminally silent or have taken most uncatholic and inhuman attitudes to the problem.

We need not spend time on that long litany of the wrong people. From the dirty-mouthed youngster who rehearses in gutter language what he has mislearned about sex, to the suave university professor, cool in his impersonal detachment, who reminds his students that they are animals and that therefore they should not be surprised at beastly inclinations or shocked or unnecessarily disturbed about the sex lapses of the animal man, young people have listened to a continued chorus of misleaders. We Catholics have hesitated to give young people instruction on matters of sex; the enemies of youth have taken the keenest delight in injecting misinformation, dirt, immoral provocation, and smart seduction into the minds and hearts of modern young people.

And so long as the false philosophy and the cheap science of our age persists in treating man as a slightly improved brother of the anthropoid ape, we cannot be surprised that the sexual act is regarded as beastly or as vulgarly funny.

But the Catholic guides of youth, perhaps in revolt or in revulsion from the attitude of the enemy, have themselves been rather guilty in another way. They became tired, and quite naturally tired, of the fact that everybody was talking sex. When many years ago Agnes Repplier bemoaned the Repeal of Reticence, she echoed the sentiments of thousands of decent people. And decent people, because they heard everybody talk it, decided to talk sex not at all. Because wrong-notioned people wanted to tell youth about sex, decent people decided that the proper course was to tell youth nothing about sex, not even the right things. Decent people met the dirty-mouthed with silence. They thought to counteract false information with no information at all.

If the blatant presentation of sin forced decent people to discuss sex and its consequence, they approached the whole matter with a shiver of horror and confined their discussion almost entirely to the sins of sex. Sex was an ugly thing. The sins against purity were horrible and swinish. The consequences of impurity were devastating. "Don't be impure," they pleaded. "See how ugly and filthy are the sins against the holy virtue." And when they said "the holy virtue," they had said just about all they intended to say on the subject of purity. Impurity became a favorite subject for retreats and missions. Priests thundered against it. Nuns pleaded against it. Parents shuddered at the thought that it might contaminate their children.

NOT IMPURITY

Impurity took the center of the stage, and purity was pushed back into an obscure and only vaguely-perceived shadow. No wonder that a great many young people began to think of impurity as a very robust and exciting thing and of purity as a shy and timid virtue whose existence could be sustained only within the vine-clad walls of a cloister, with the nourishment of bread and water, and with the protection of the repressive hairshirt.

I am convinced that much too much has been said about impurity. I am persuaded that much good pedagogical skill has been wasted in the effort to depict the horror and ugliness of vice. And to me that negative approach seems completely wrong, for it gives to the negative and the ugly the compliment of intense concentration of attention. It shoves aside, ignores, and leaves perennially vague and misunderstood the gloriously positive and wondrously beautiful things that are manly purity and womanly virtue.

Talks on impurity are, to use our favorite current word, dynamite. It would be hard to persuade me that such talks do not have effects that are almost entirely different from the intended effects. Such talks produce disgust, disgust not so much with the subject of impurity as with the person who talks so feelingly about it. Such talks arouse a cynical question in the mind of the listener: "How does he know so confounded much about it?" Such talks produce in groups of modest people panic or a paralysis of embarrassment. Unless they are thoughtfully worked out and brilliantly presented, talks about impurity actually open vistas that had never before been glimpsed by the sheltered young listener, vistas that stimulate curiosity and that sometimes actually arouse passions.

For impurity is an unique crime in this: The bare recital of the facts is extraordinarily attractive. We give the details of a murder, and though the listeners may be fascinated, they are also repelled. We launch into a diatribe against impurity, and although our oratory creates a slight revulsion, it creates too a powerful curiosity, a stimulated fascination, an attraction that may remain long after the shudder of revulsion has gone.

From most talks on impurity the listener carries away with him one predominant idea: "Well it's certainly an interesting subject, and I suppose the main thing is to be careful."

Some years ago, when the campaign against social diseases was becoming an international one, a French play was translated into English and presented on the American stage. The play was intended to be an *exposé* of the consequences of promiscuity. Actually the moral of the play was this: "If you are going to be promiscuous, be extremely careful. Choose the right people with whom to be promiscuous." I doubt that this play had any perceptible effect upon the elimination of social diseases; I know that it did nothing to stem the tide of impurity. The play was followed by a surge of impure conduct, for the play appealed to the prurient-minded far more than it appealed to those whose hope was the betterment of human social relations.

I can recall my own youth and the recurrent talks that I heard on the subject of impurity. My reaction was one of startled, hushed, and nervous excitement. Any public speaker or guide of youth knows exactly what happens in an audience of young people when the subject of impurity is mentioned. The audience grows preternaturally silent. You can feel the quiet. It is as if every boy and every girl in the audience had congealed into a composite block of concentrated attention. There isn't a sound as they sit, all of them, ears alert, mind fully awake and watching and listening and drinking in your words.

I well remember a certain occasion on which an excellent and sincerely interested priest gave us his one and only talk on sex. It was long before the fact of social disease had became public discussion, and his talk was on the loathesome consequences of sexual sins. He described a soldier in the advanced stage of syphilis who was exposed to the scrutiny of all the men in his regiment. He launched into long arguments against any dealings with immoral women, arguments based only on the consequences that such dealings had on health.

Well when the talk was over, I felt more than a little sick. The district between my school and the station of the elevated railroad that carried me home was one known to be inhabited by prostitutes. I walked to the station with a new interest in this district; I was curious about these women who were such carriers of disease. Sex itself took on for me a stench and an aura of horror. Seated in the train, I looked curiously at a pale, sickly young man who was seated opposite me and wondered whether or not he had a social disease. For the first time I noticed advertisements for certain medicines.

I learned that in our city there was a museum given over to charts and figures of the spread of social diseases through the activities of quack doctors, who actually innoculated guileless boys and young men with the germs; that museum became a source of morbid curiosity for me.

And when later on I learned that social diseases could be warded off, my only remaining reaction to that first talk was that of sheer disgust.

To launch into attacks upon impurity is in most instances to waste time. At best an attack upon impurity is a plea to youth to be careful. And when has youth ever given a snap of its slim fingers for the questionable virtue of carefulness?

But Purity Is Glorious

What youth has seldom been told is that purity is a glorious thing. Until the glory of purity is demonstrated to youth in clearest language, sex instruction is wasted.

The whole matter of sex guidance, the whole question of boy-and-girl association must center on the highest possible ideals of purity. Those ideals can be lifted to exalted heights; sex can be made to seem what it is, one of the great God-given powers with which the creator has endowed His creatures.

In other words let's declare a moratorium on talks about impurity. And let's talk purity to our young people; let's talk it in ringing tones and with glowing eyes. Then we may make a real impression on them. Then we can hope to develop clean minds in clean bodies.

Here briefly is what I believe is the correct approach to use in speaking to young people about sex.

1. Purity is not a negative virtue.

The enemies of purity have of course used the argument that purity is a negative virtue. Those enemies have pictured the pure as weaklings. They have described the impure as ruddy, manly men and fascinating, daring women. They have classed chastity with meekness and forgiveness of enemies, and they have condemned all of the virtues with the epithet cowardly. They have painted the chaste man as pale and the chaste woman as essentially a colorless flower.

Purity is really agressively, gloriously positive. It is a virtue to be classed with the courage of martyrs and the zeal of the missionaries. Like courage and zeal, purity is intimately connected with life and the safe and beautiful increase of life. It is not a renunciation. It is a knightly virtue that strikes down those who would lay ugly hands on women or soiled hands on children. It is akin to that splendid Christian attitude which as the ship begins to sink prompts the cry, "Women and children first!"

Why?

2. Because purity is a strong protective safeguard which the brave and the clear-seeing man throws around the great creative power.

Man and woman together have been endowed with the glorious power of bringing into the world a third human being, a baby, who has a place of enormous importance in this world and a destiny to immortality in the world to come. Only through the correct use of this creative power can children enter the world. If the power is correctly used, children are born safely and happily. If the power is basely or selfishly used, the consequence falls less on the guilty parties—though they too may suffer—than on the child, who is the God-ordained consequence of all sexual acts.

Man and woman then are the joint custodians of a simply incredible power, the power of calling other men into existence. With that power is linked the cooperating act by which God creates a human and immortal soul to inhabit the body that the joint action of husband and wife has conceived in the wife's womb. Man becomes a father. Woman becomes the dearest thing in the world, a mother. And God enters into association with His sons and daughters by creating the soul to inhabit the body that they have conceived through the use of the power of sex.

3. This creative power makes men and women Godlike.

God's supreme prerogative is the prerogative of creation. He calls the world into being by His compelling fiat. He fashions men and women to His image and likeness and breathes into their bodies a living soul.

God could quite easily have continued to people the world simply by repeating that act with which He lifted Adam from the dust. God could have remained the sole creator.

This He did not do. He chose to share His great personal characteristics with His creature man, whom He endowed with intellect, free will, immortality. And He shares too the great power of creation. More than that; He may almost be said to stand back and wait until man uses his creative power correctly and splendidly.

Purity then is simply the intelligent attitude which prompts a man or a woman to say: "I shall use this creative power of sex only as God meant me to use it. It is God's creative power expressed in terms of my human limitations. Never will I do anything that will thwart this creative power. Certainly I shall never use this power in a way that will destroy its purpose and prevent the birth of those children whom God wants but who must wait upon my free cooperation with Him."

4. For the pure man realizes that only through the correct use of this power can God's children be brought safely and decently into the world.

Children must be born. Heaven must be filled. The affairs of earth must be carried forward. There will be under God's providence men and women who by vow will consecrate this power of sexual creation to God so that they may give their whole lives, not to children of their own, but to the children of others who may call upon them. But unless men and women exercise this power correctly, children will not be born or will be born sick, soiled, half-thwarted from the time of conception; heaven will not be filled with happy citizens; the business of the world will go undone or will fall into weak and incompetent hands.

So the pure man safeguards the power of sexual creation simply because it is the power on which depends the entire future of this world and the next. Such a tremendous power is not something to use selfishly. Certainly it is nothing to laugh about. Abuse of a thing like that is the weak betrayal of one of man's highest responsibilities. God has entrusted to men the whole future of the race, and the pure man says, bravely, "I shall try to be worthy of that trust."

All the while the pure man realizes that the wolves of the world, fangs bared, are attacking this unborn future. He sees the prostitute as a woman who substitutes the brute desires of passion for the glory of motherhood. He sees the *roué* or the libertine as a villain who uses his God-given power to betray the innocent, to spoil the lives of the weak, and to substitute his own animal satisfaction for the fulfillment of his creative destiny. And the pure man sees himself as standing with his arms protectingly outstretched between these wolves who would tear the future to pieces and the women who should be mothers and the children who must be safely born. The pure young woman sees herself as the one gateway through which can pass that section of the future which was intended to flow safely and splendidly through her pure body.

How in the world can any man or woman in his right senses fail to see how splendidly positive is the virtue of purity?

5. The woman who bears children and the parents who must bring those children through difficult years to full manhood and womanhood assume a heavy burden; therefore God offers to them a great reward: love.

God always rewards every good action of man. He even repays man for the fulfillment of his instincts. Man has a thirst for knowledge; wisdom and experience are man's reward. Man must keep his own life sound and strong, and to do this he must eat; the delights of food are actually God's rewards to man for preserving his life. God must wait upon man for the production of further life; that production of life and the consequent rearing of children will entail great sacrifices and hardships. But God rewards men for bringing new life into the world; He gives men and women a powerful and delightful attraction for one another, that ennobling emotional experience that we call love. God envelopes in the ecstatic pleasure of passion the actual moment in which life can be conceived.

So the pure man sees that attraction, love, and passion are all one with the central idea of new life. They are the reward that God gives him for facing the responsibilities of parenthood. They may result in fine things for him personally. They are primarily and by their nature God's return to him for cooperating with the creator in the peopling of the world.

6. Hence sin against this power is really a betrayal of God and a betrayal of the future.

Any act of impurity is a betrayal. When an unmarried man and woman accept the act of love and passion, which was meant to be man's way of cooperating with God's creative desires, they take the act merely for the pleasure; they risk children's being born into the world without decent protections and safeguards; they betray God's trust; they cheat by taking what they have not earned.

Birth control is a system of pagan practice by which men and women say: "We will accept, O God, the delights of sex, those delights which you meant to be our reward for the fulfillment of our creative power. But we will not fulfill that creative power. We will take the delights and deny you the natural consequences of that delight. We will have our own selfish joy, but we will not give you new life. We will steal happiness for ourselves and give you nothing in return. We will accept our wage but decline to do our appointed task."

All those sins which attempt to make of sex something vulgar or funny or indecent are a little like sacrileges. They are the betrayal or the mocking of a sacred, most important thing. They are inhuman and antihuman. They scoff at the only way by which human life can be produced. They disgrace and pull down that guarded gateway through which humanity must enter this world and the kingdom of God.

In Summary

The summarized argument, the outlined presentation of this whole matter in its positive and idealistic aspect would run thus:

1. Purity is not a negative virtue;

2. But it is the strong protection which a clear-seeing and strong-willed man and woman

3. Throw around the great creative power, upon the correct use of which depends the whole future;

4. A power entrusted by the creator to His children

5. As the means for peopling earth and filling heaven.

6. This power, because it demands hard things in the long and tedious bearing and training of children, is, when properly exercised, rewarded by God, and that reward is mutual attraction, love, and passion.

7. God, as every Catholic very well knows, thought all this sufficiently important to consecrate it with a sacrament.

8. Hence sin against this power is terrible because:

a. It betrays the creative power and imperils the whole future.

b. It steals the rewards of love without accepting the responsibilities for which those rewards were given.

THESE THINGS FOLLOW

I am convinced that most people talk badly when they talk about impurity. They say too much, and thus they amuse the cynical. Or they say too little, and thus they puzzle the innocent.

But I am convinced that any intelligent counselor of youth who will follow this outline and use the approach here indicated can give talks or instructions on purity and offend no one, excite no prurient curiosity, and arouse high ideals and noble impulses. Surely a priest can do it easily. A religious brother could effectively handle this subject, just because of the elevated character of his own vow of chastity.

And a calm, common-sense nun could give these talks without offending her modesty in the slightest degree, without inspiring in her students anything except increased respect.

But note how different this positive approach is from the violent attacks on impurity, the dingy details and the ugly innuendoes that must accompany any talk on vice. It is a gloriously easy and inspiring thing to talk about purity. Only a great saint should be allowed to talk on impurity, and he probably would be so busy praising purity that he wouldn't find time for a discussion of the distasteful offenses against one of God's greatest gifts to men.

Young people are impressed when they are brought to realize that purity is an endowment of the strong and that strength is found in the pure of heart. "His strength was as the strength of ten because his heart was pure," was Tennyson's way of stating a truism. When a man or a woman is pure, he or she can be trusted. Youth sees that at once. Youth sees that you can place a pure man or woman in any position and he or she will come through with the proverbial flying colors. The pure man won't be deflected from his line of duty by the pull of passion; he won't betray a great cause for some hot-lipped woman. The pure woman won't walk out on her duty because some man beckons; she won't break homes or hearts or pacts or pledges, just because her selfishness calls her to fling aside everything else at the call of passion. You need only indicate this to young people. They see it clearly.

On the other hand no one, no matter how brilliant his arguments have been, has ever really convinced young people that the lustful person is not a weak person. Young people from their own experience have learned that when they are strong they say no to temptation; that when they are weak, temptation has its own way with them. They can understand and appreciate the plain story of men's betrayal of great issues for the interest of petty loves: Napoleon's leading his army to Russia and collapse because he was too busy gratifying his love for a mistress to be the usual master of strategy; Parnell's leaving his country at the time of near-victory because of his desire for a woman.

They know that a man who has regularly given in to his passions soon becomes so weak that he can be trusted nowhere and with no one. They know that a picture in a window, a stray gust of wind, a wandering eye is temptation enough to lead such a man straight into a betrayal of his creative power. Young people need only be reminded that the strong man is the man who has mastered himself. Any weak fool can run into temptation with open arms and take seductive passion to his heart; only a strong man has the courage to resist.

CONSEQUENCES

I have perhaps spent too much time on the subject of this constructive attitude toward sex, but I am convinced that if this attitude were ingrained in our children and young people there would be no real boy-and-girl problem. All the idealism of correct standards of morality flows from the correct attitude. Chivalry is born of it. Self-respect flowers from this magnificent ideal.

The young person who once sees sex as an essential power on which rests the future, a power which is Godlike in its creative effects, a power that is rewarded by God in abounding fashion—such a young person will gladly follow the counselor as that counselor points out the correlaries of this viewpoint.

That young person sees immediately why he must have deep respect for the opposite sex. Each man and each woman is the bearer of a life germ. As such he or she is the sanctuary of the future. From that man and that woman will come either a wholesome and sound generation or a generation that is spoiled before it is conceived, twisted and soiled before it is born.

Self-respect is the inevitable result of this realization. For the young man can say: "I am a carrier of life. I am a potential father." The young woman can realize that her body is the fountain from which will flow the future. Knowing this, how can they do other than regard themselves as precious and important to both God and man?

Love becomes a sacred thing. Love is not the casual relationship between two animals, nor is it the temporary attachment formed by silly young things who go off their heads at the sight of golden hair or smiling eyes. Love is the glorious reward that God has established for the difficult career of parenthood. It is God's sanction on the use of the creative act.

Marriage becomes a career. Men and women enter into a partnership with God Himself; and in marriage the husband and the wife and the almighty creator cooperate in the production of the little baby that snuggles against its mother's breast. Seeing marriage as so sacred and noble a thing, the young boy and young girl are quick to see why they cannot risk its success by wasting affection on the casual partner of a dance. They see that they must prepare for the career of marriage prayerfully and purposefully, just as a man prepares for any career of real importance. They will have to save for the partner who is to help them make that career a success all the love they can hold in their hearts. They would be fools to pour that love out on the person with whom they have done no more than share a hamburger.

Correct manners come straight from respect. Mutual respect can be most effectively generated by placing on a plane of high ideals the relationship between men and women. Modesty is not prudery. The human instinct is to cover from vulgar or indecent eyes anything which is sacred. The priest goes to the altar with the chalice veiled; it would not be quite right if the vessel which is to hold the blood of the Savior were the object of vulgar curiosity. Christian convention veils the body of a woman simply because that body is the chalice which God has shaped to hold the precious life of an unborn baby.

Are bodies to be regarded with contempt and dislike? On the contrary; they are to be regarded as beautiful and precious. God made them beautiful because they have so high and noble a purpose. They are precious because they carry life and produce life.

THE HANDLING OF THE SUBJECT

This whole matter of the boy-and-girl relationship can be handled in a series of straightforward talks. In all cases the simplest audience to address is a one-sex audience. A group of boys are attentive and respectful. A group of girls are alert and interested. With slight differences in approach talks to either group can be made quite pleasant and easy.

Yet it is my experience that a talk can be adequately given to a mixed group as well. In retreats I have faced small and large audiences made up of both sexes. I found no embarrassment and no nervousness on their part when I handled sex from its constructive and positive side. I should have been in a dither, and I'm sure they would have been on edge, had I talked on impurity and vice to that same mixed audience.

So any fairly intelligent and competent guide of youth can, when the need arises or the opportunity presents itself, handle this subject. This is true of priests, religious brothers, and teaching nuns alike.

Let this be noted however. People can easily grow obsessed with the subject of sex. And by people I mean decent and quite holy people. They can get to the point where they drag sex into everything; that attitude is undoubtedly greatly mistaken. The subject of sex should be treated in a talk or a connected series of talks. It should then be dropped completely. Harking back to it, diluting it over a long period of time, dragging it into all sorts of subjects and discussions—this creates a notoriously bad impression. The listeners grow convinced that their counselor thinks much too much about the subject. And the subject, dulled by repeated treatment, comes to mean nothing or, worse still, becomes the subject for covert laughter and sneers.

Booklets or books to supplement the talks may be given the young people. Most of the books published by the secular press are animalistic in their treatment of this subject. Life is not precious to the authors of these books, for life cannot be precious to anyone who sees it as no more than a brief and unintelligible flash of light between two darknesses. Such authors cannot have a true Christian respect for love or birth or the education of children. They miss the whole glorious point of the cooperation of parents with God, the creator.

Yet some few of these books do have chapters which are excellent. The counselor of youth will read them and use them as his wisdom dictates.

The Catholic literature on the subject has grown within the last few years. These Catholic books and booklets—after they have been read by the counselor—can be given to young people who want something in print to add to the instructions given.

What is most needed perhaps is cooperation between parents and those others who are responsible for youth's guidance. Especially should the parents of very young children be taught the complete approach to sex instruction. For parents are, as I have repeated monotonously, the natural guides of youth. If we counselors are doing our full duty, we are insistently shifting the burden of sex instructions, even along the lines I have indicated, from our own shoulders to the shoulders of the parents. But a gesture or a shrug will not accomplish this transfer. The transfer can be accomplished only when we have taught the parents how to handle the subject of sex and how to make the proper approach to the problems of their children.

THINGS TO AVOID

When we talk with young people on subjects of sex, we must remember that rule one is this: Never appear to be shocked by anything you may have to say or by anything that they may want to ask.

There is nothing evil or shocking about sex. The only horror about sex is that which comes when vice betrays so noble and important a power. Hence the subject should be approached with perfect calm of mind and perfect serenity of exterior.

Then there is a second rule: We must never act as if young people in general were bad or as if this young person in particular were hopeless. Such action is fatal. When temptation first lays siege to the young soul, the young person involved has a moment of frightful distrust: Can it be, he wonders, that he is queer or perverted or so essentially evil that he is beyond salvation? If he reads in the attitude of his counselor anything that even slightly confirms his own suspicion, he is inclined to surrender to the temptation without a struggle. Why fight when a traitor within himself is powerfully linked with the forces of evil without?

A counselor's regarding young people in general as pretty bad alienates young people, even when the counselor does not mean to include present company in his general indictment. Young people are not hopeless. They are not even pretty bad. But if they were, what can we do save work for them out of love and devoted affection?

Time was when the way of treating any discussion of sex was to introduce lighted candles and an attitude of deep, awed mystery. "Come, little one, and sit down at my feet while, with violins playing 'Hearts and Flowers' and pink candles throwing soft light over the scene, I tell you about the bees and the pollen."

The hushed and mysterious approach to sex is out! That approach sets the youngsters' nerves on edge. It creates a fictitious atmosphere that stimulates and arouses emotional reactions—usually the wrong reactions. It makes the whole subject of sex seem something a little dreadful. It puts the discussion on an unnatural, strained, artificial plane. It creates unnecessary vibrations. It results in emotional overemphasis.

The more matter-of-fact the tone, the better. The fewer the pink candles and the less hushed the voices, the better. Sex is a sacred subject, but it is not an awesome one. While essentially intimate, it concerns the whole human race. The top of a bus would be a better spot for a father and son to talk things over than is that dimly-lighted space before the fireplace, where the son sits nervously on the edge of a hassock and the father lowers his voice to sepulchral whispers.

The most effective setting for a group discussion that was ever presented to me was one I found not long after I began my priestly work. A sister principal had reason to believe that a certain group of girls in the senior high-school class were curious about sex and perhaps wiser than their years in the matter. She asked me to give them a talk on purity and sex. She arranged the setting quite simply. I came out to the school after class. The girls were merely told that I was giving them a talk, subject unknown. When I arrived, they were gathered in their very comfortable recreation room, playing the piano and singing popular songs. The sister introduced me, and the music went on for a while. Then we drifted away from the piano and sat down in some easy chairs. Some of them, I remember, sat on the floor. Then without preamble beyond, "Sister thought you might be interested in getting a fairly complete and consecutive story of this mysterious thing called love," I talked for an hour.

"Any questions?" I concluded. And they asked me questions for an hour and a quarter.

Then we got up, and without the slightest sign of self-consciousness they drifted back to the piano and resumed their music. I'll admit though that the influence of that particular nun was extraordinary, and her power over her girls was altogether unusual and wholesome.

Counselors make a frightful mistake if their attitude shows even slightly that they regard love or marriage or sex as unpleasant themes. Far, far worse is it however when they clearly indicate that they regard these themes as unpleasant or evil. If a counselor cannot get over that attitude, he should never speak to young people about the subjects. Evidences of that attitude will creep into his talks and spoil whatever he may have to say.

TALKING THROUGH

In this subject, as in all individual problems, the wise counselor encourages his young friends to talk freely. He encourages them to disagree. And when they have begun the statement of a problem, he lets them finish that statement completely and without interruption. His answer to the problem is given along the lines we have indicated. He does not minimize evil. He does not say, "Well that really doesn't matter." But he talks as little of the evil as possible, and he stresses virtue and goodness. If he speaks of evil, he speaks of it only in so far as it is a betrayal of virtue and goodness. Young people hate traitors. They are repelled from any course of action which makes them betray things that are sacred or beautiful.

DON'T ASSOCIATE TOTALLY DIFFERENT THINGS

Said a certain sister dean to me: "There's one thing we're proud of. None of the girls of our college smoke or drink or run around in coupés with strange men or go off on week ends without our knowing where they are."

I answered: "Very good indeed, sister. But I sincerely hope that you never put it exactly that way to your girls."

She looked her surprise.

"It would," I explained, "be a great mistake to have them think that you grouped smoking, drinking, strange men in coupés, and unsupervised week ends all in the same category."

This is of course exactly what a great many guides of youth do. They thereby create false standards for their young people, or, what is even more disastrous, they make the young people totally distrustful of their counselors' judgment. For whatever you may think of smoking, smoking and drinking are by no means parallel habits; and to class smoking with running around with strange men is as stupid as to class the drinking of a mild highball and the spending of a week end in a big hotel as equally grave things.

Things which are sins should be treated as sins. But things which are sins should not be massed together in one sweeping condemnation with things which are not sins. That confuses the issue. It makes the youngster feel that we do not distinguish between things which are sinful and things which may be merely common, between things which are perhaps dangerous and things which are clearly wrong.

Prudes are the last people in the world who should have anything to do with young people. And a prude is a person who sees evil where evil does not exist. Prudes are alarmed by dancing, which in nine hundred and ninety-nine cases out of a thousand is, among decent young people, quite free from even danger. Any new fad or fashion upsets the prude. I can remember when the girls' schools of the country were threatening wholesale expulsion because girls had started to bob their hair. Not too remote is the day when a cigarette in the mouth of a boy was regarded by certain priests as only slightly less horrible than a needle shot in the arm.

The person who upholds standards and is proud of traditions is glorious. But the person who creates false standards and sticks to merely conventional traditions, however beautiful, as if they were things graven on tablets of stone is simply stupid. Sins are sins, and conventions are conventions, and though the twain may sometimes meet, only a prude gets them so confused that he thinks that the convention is the virtue and the violation of the convention is the sin. And when a counselor takes the prudish attitude with young people, they know instinctively that he is wrong, and either they are troubled in conscience or they lose their respect for his judgment.

Prudes are the enemies of purity. They make virtue ridiculous. They create false consciences. They can't judge for themselves, so certainly they should not be allowed to judge for others. They see so much evil in normal conduct that they make the youngster despair of ever being even mildly good. They think of evil when they should be seeing virtue. They dread vice when they should be praising goodness. They induce despair when they should be creating ideals.

Let Them Talk

If a counselor has once established the constructive basis for purity in his consultant, he is safe in trusting the youngster's own decisions pretty far. In fact he is wise to encourage the youngster to form his own conscience—under the counselor's guiding eye of course—and to give the counselor his own solution to the problems.

Youngsters will. They will tell the counselor just why a dirty story is evil. They will see that it a shameful thing to laugh at the way life enters the world and to besmirch with ridicule the love which is God's reward for the career of parenthood.

They will be able to tell him why an obscene magazine is a villainous thing and why an off-color show is treason to man's highest interests. Immodesty takes on for them its clear significance and loses its sensuous appeal. They know why immodesty is dangerous and evil. They see its connection with the great betrayal of love.

And when the modern immoralist presents his brilliant and persuasive arguments for promiscuity and lax conduct, these youngsters will have the answer clearly in their minds and their hearts. They will lose the feeling that they are missing something by being pure. They will not regard themselves as weak and the immoralist as strong. They will clearly see themselves as the brave defenders of one of man's most precious powers and important trusts. And that very conviction of their own dignity will be the strongest answer they can give to the enemies of chastity.

Young people should be encouraged to present the reasons for modesty, for decency, for the importance of safeguarding themselves, for the high responsibility of safeguarding one another. Ordinarily they would talk hesitatingly and with embarrassment about impurity, but they will find no embarrassment in unhesitatingly stating the case for purity. And the more often young people themselves state the case for purity, the more sure we can be that they are facing the problem of purity with clear eyes and from an intelligent viewpoint.

THE DESIRE FOR COMPANIONSHIP

The average little girl regards boys as complete nuisances. The average little boy regards girls as complete nuisances. This means that during the early days each prefers companions of his own sex. Little boys like to go with little boys. Little girls enjoy being with little girls. Little boys and little girls barely tolerate one another.

Even during long periods throughout their adolescence girls and boys may prefer to stay by themselves rather than go about too frequently in mixed groups. Athletics are as a rule one-sex affairs. And athletics have, we may say with great gratitude, filled large sectors of the lives of our growing boys. The girls' club is a natural thing. And girls in clubs are surprisingly content with the companionship of other girls.

All this I state merely because I should not want to seem to force boys and girls on one another at times when they are quite content to be alone. The average boy prefers a tennis game with his fellows to a set of mixed doubles. The average girl prefers to belong to a card club made up of girls rather than to join a club in which boys will prevent the normal activities which girls enjoy.

But the natural desire for companionship that exists in all young hearts must be taken into consideration. There are times when young people of opposite sex rightly like to be together, rightly want to be together. A young person is naturally drawn toward companions of the other sex. There are sports and games that are best played by boys and girls together. And the Catholic guides and counselors of youth are making a mistake if they do not provide the chance for this mixed social life.

When I was in high school, some of my professors acted as if only a sissy paid any attention to girls. Girls were treated with an air that suggested that they were silly, unimportant, frivolous, probably slightly evil, and certainly dangerous. I don't think the attitude was good. I know that it made some of the boys furtive in their attitude toward girls. And I know there was much clandestine association, which was certainly far from wholesome.

That school which encourages and supervises a certain amount of pleasant social contact between boys and girls is acting wisely. A boarding school that completely segregates boys from girls and girls from boys is following a decidedly doubtful course. One convent school that we young fellows knew well during my high-school and college days kept their boarders so tightly cloistered during the school year that we used to say: "During the holidays the girls from that school fall in love with the first messenger boy they see on the street." And there was some truth in the statement.

Association under pleasant auspices makes for the moral safety of young people. That association is best provided by the parents. But the school can take a hand. And boarding schools should make it possible. I find something a little ridiculous in the men's or women's boarding college that frowns on mixed gatherings. I remember with something like horror the first time that I heard that in one men's boarding college some of the boys dressed as girls and danced with the other boys, for girls were not permitted on the campus.

College life has kept boys and girls in school long past the years when they are quite matured. Our mothers and fathers were married and rearing a family at an age when our modern young men and young women are just entering the sophomore class in college. It is true that this prolonged education has protracted adolescence somewhat. But it is also true that some schools bottle up the social nature of their students to the explosive point. The fact that the course of studies has been lengthened has not essentially altered human development. Many a modern boy who is a college freshman would, if he had been that same age half a century ago, have been entering matrimony, not a class in fundamental English literature.

So teas to which the members of the other sex are invited are quite in line with what I think should be routine in our Catholic one-sex colleges. Evenings when young men can call or afternoons when they can freely meet the girls on the campus seem only the natural thing. I think parties today are necessary and right, just as I thought parties were necessary and right when I was a youngster. A well-rounded social life is an essential part of the development of the upper high-school classes; certainly it is essential for the college students. I am inclined very much to doubt the benefits of coeducation; I am certain that I like and approve of pleasant and happily supervised social relationships.

Students, and we can stick to them for just a minute, see nothing incongruous in making religion dominate their social life. In fact the thing they find illogical is that certain religious people try to separate completely the social life of young people from their religion.

I have in speeches repeatedly told young people about the formal dance given by a certain great Catholic university, and I have always found my recital greeted with undisguised approval. At that particular dance the students chose Our Lady's blue and white for their decorative scheme. They placed her statue at the hall's most central point and built the decorations around the statue. The formal opening march led to that statue. The marchers, dressed in evening clothes, knelt on the ballroom floor. The leaders of the grand march, a young man and a young woman, then went up to the statue; the girl crowned Our Lady; the young man consecrated the dancers to the queen of our social life. The dancers all echoed the consecration in a heartfelt amen. The first number by the orchestra was a waltz dedicated to Our Lady. And the party went on under her auspices.

May I say that that dance set a high standard for that university? And may I also say that when I have talked to young people about this particular party I have found them unanimously approving?

Young people are social by nature. They want to go with those of the opposite sex. They are a little worried when their social life seems to fall under the disapproving eye of religious men and women. They feel furtive if religion gives no blessing to their gregarious nature. And when any slightest element of religion can rest approvingly on their gayety, they love it and welcome it with deepest enthusiasm.

During the course of one of our very first Sodality conventions we brought our student delegates together for a party. At the conclusion of the party a sudden and unpremediated impulse brought me to the center of the hall, and I said: "Let's all kneel for night prayers." They did, kneeling down on the dance floor with quick reverence. The next night saw the convention's closing banquet. When that banquet had been ended and the final grace had been said, a delegation of the Sodalists came up to me. "How about night prayers?" they demanded. And I saw that they really wanted to say them.

Since that time we have ended all social gatherings, whatever their nature—parties, dances, amateur nights, plays, entertainments—by asking the young people to kneel and say their night prayers together. I have yet to hear even a slight echo of youthful disapproval. Instead we have found that they welcome this wedding of their religious and their social natures with unmixed enthusiasm and an attitude that plainly says: "Of course that is just what we should always do."

The Parish as the Center

Gratefully I remember how, in my not too distant youth, home and the parish were the centers of my social life. My mother, bless her, believed that her house was the place where we should be our gayest. And we were. I lived successively in two Chicago parishes. Fortunately each of them believed in making life socially pleasant for the young people. We loved our parish church for the Mass and the sacraments that came to us through it. But we also turned to our parish church for the wholesome and delightful social life that it afforded us.

We had our dramatic society, out of which came a surprising number of Catholic marriages. We had our choir, that rehearsed in the home of our choir directress and brought young people together in delightful association. After the rehearsal for the Mass for Christmas was ended, we sang with equal enthusiasm and equal blending of sopranos and basses, of tenors and altos, the popular songs of the day. We picnicked under church auspices. Our parish hall was the center of a continuous social life. We had no need for the public dance hall. We felt little attraction for places which might have been dangerous to our morals. We turned to the parish, for the parish was the center of our active recreational life.

And I cannot recall having seen or taken part in any action or having heard of any action that would have brought shame to the most fastidious defender of Catholic morality. Because we had our good times under the smiling eyes of our priests and in the shadow of the church, these good times were astoundingly free, not only from sin, but from even the most distant approach of evil.

Young people want to be together. The Church pleads for Catholic marriages and deplores mixed marriages. Then logically it is the task of our Catholic guides and counselors to see to it that Catholic young people have a chance to meet and by happy association to prepare for Catholic marriage and the Catholic home. Churchmen may insulate young men from young women, but those young men will still find young women—women perhaps altogether unacceptable to Catholic practice. If young women do not get a chance to meet Catholic young men under wholesome auspices, are they to be blamed if they linger on as old maids or if they accept from young men not of their faith the attentions which their nature craves? The rules of the Church on the subject of mixed marriages are magnificent. But in a country like ours, where Catholics are outnumbered by more than four to one, young Catholics stand an excellent chance of meeting four non-Catholics for every one Catholic they meet.

Unless the Catholic school fosters a wholesome social life . . .

Unless the Catholic home opens its doors to the Catholic friends of its sons and daughters . . .

Unless the Catholic parish becomes the center to which Catholic young people can turn in the confident hope that under safe and happy auspices churchmen will make it possible for them to meet the sort of people of whom the Church can officially approve . . .

Unless these things come to pass, the problems of mixed marriage will continue.

The mixed-marriage problem is one of simple arithmetic: We Catholics are outnumbered four to one. If we stay in that ratio, the chance that Catholics will marry those of their own faith is one in four. The ratio must be rebalanced by a social life in which Catholic young people meet other Catholic young people almost exclusively. Marriages come out of social life. We can completely destroy the four-to-one ratio by a social life that is entirely Catholic. All the sermons and headshakings and pastoral letters won't readjust the mathematics of four to one. A well organized social life does readjust it and always will.

All of which I present as serious matter for thought for us priests and religious who say we have at heart the interests, present and future, of our young people.

For Chaperones

I am quite aware that for many reasons, natural and ecclesiastical, priests and religious cannot spend a great deal of time in the actual supervision of the young people's social life. The religious have a few more things to do.

But social life must go on. And we must still to some extent inaugurate it.

That is where we can call upon our older Catholics to handle under our wise guidance the future of our younger Catholics. We can initiate what the Catholic lay man and lay woman can carry through. We can plan what they can execute.

One grand pastor, for whom I have a sort of reverent respect, had a church, a good hall, a fine parish, and a large number of neglected young people. Of course the faithful few belonged to his select church organizations for the young. The majority gravitated to the neighboring motion-picture theaters and to the big dance palace, which was some two blocks away from the very center of the parish.

But this pastor also had an understanding heart and an excellent ushers' society. He had bound those ushers to him by the simple expedient of giving them breakfast on the Sunday mornings that they tended the crowds at Mass. Now he had a new job for them. He turned over to them the management of the social life of the young people of the parish.

The ushers promptly organized two committees: one for the door; one for the floor. They took the parish hall as their center of activities. They hired an excellent orchestra. They laid down a few simple rules, chief among which was the rule that parties started at eight and ended slightly before midnight. They launched the social life of the parish.

During the first winter of the development of this project a weekly average of five hundred and fifty young people met for the parties. The dance palace went into a sharp decline. The young people of the parish came to know one another as they had never known each other before. The other societies of the parish took new leases on life. And the wise old pastor scarcely had to leave his study. He did the thinking and the planning. The laymen carried everything into effect.

Priests and brothers and sisters can hardly operate dance halls or supervise parties. But aren't we constantly being told that the world is full of earnest and competent lay men and lay women who are looking for the opportunity to foster Catholic activities? I know diocesan councils of Catholic women that are wasting their time thumb-twiddling when they could, with hardly an effort and with no expense to themselves, initiate and carry through magnificent social programs for young people. I know alumnae associations that sit around lamenting that they haven't any money and haven't any work to do. And they could be handling all the details of fostering and chaperoning the social life of their schools. Parents weep futile tears because they feel themselves remote from their young people. How about getting together with a few more Catholic parents and establishing a neighborhood social life for these youngsters of theirs?

There's too much headshaking over young people. What young people need is not headshaking but handclasping. They need less despair and more dances. They are waiting for their elders' organizations to give them the chance to exercise their youthful gayety under decent auspices. The purveyors of evil are quite willing to put themselves out to accommodate youth. The guardians of good are reluctant to disturb their calm evenings long enough to provide and supervise the recreations of their own sons and daughters.

If priests and nuns will encourage the older people of the parish to work for the younger people, Catholic recreational life will flourish, and it will not be necessary for the priest to supervise dances, and the nuns will not get circles under their eyes from sitting up and waiting for latecomers to return from the parties.

COMMON QUESTIONS

The most frequent question that a girl asks a priest or a sister in whom she can confide is this:

"Is it a sin to let a boy kiss me?"

Please note the way in which that question is asked. Never does she ask: "Is it a sin for me to kiss a boy?" or "Is it a sin to kiss a boy?" She puts it passively: "Is it a sin to let a boy kiss me?" She indicates her purely receptive and non-aggressive part in the whole affair. And that, I think, is the quite characteristic attitude of good girls.

The answer, I believe, should take the discussion right out of the realm of sin. The stress should be, not upon sin, but upon the girl's high responsibilities for the future, upon the kiss as a symbol of love, upon the sacredness of love in its connection with marriage, and upon the fact that some day a kiss will be the one sign by which she can prove to a young man that she loves him well enough to bind herself to him for life.

Girls are impressed when they understand the symbolism of a kiss, its token of surrender, its consecration, its use as a symbol of that love which cements two lives together in the great career of matrimony. They are quick too to see the vulgarity of the promiscuous kiss. Custom has very much staled the kiss. But custom can never destroy a girl's instinctive realization that the kiss is something very sacred and very beautiful, that the kiss is a surrender of herself and her affection to someone who has won more than a transient place in her affections.

Girls can be shown too that free and easy kissing brings about a definite degree of "shopwornness." The girl who is too easily kissed is too obviously secondhand. Boys know that too. They have an innate contempt for the girl who is easy and loose, even about kissing. They may like the kiss and take it greedily, but they have a quick contempt for the girl who grants it easily after a chocolate sundae at the corner drug store. The kiss is an expensive price to pay a boy for some trifling treat.

All this can easily be made clear to a girl, and she readily understands it.

The approach to the possible sinfulness of kissing should, I think, be handled through questions. It is better to make the girl give an answer than to give her the answer all tailor-made. When the question has been asked me, I have talked about the sacredness of the symbol which is a kiss. And then I have asked the following questions:

"You want to know whether or not it is sinful to let a boy kiss you. Well that includes the question: Is a kiss sinful? Let's suppose a mother kisses her child? Sinful?"

Almost relieved at the apparent frivolity of the question, she answers, promptly: "Of course not, father."

"If a brother affectionately kisses his sister when she leaves for a holiday, is that a sin?"

Again her laughter.

"It may be unusual, but it's not a sin."

"So then a kiss in itself may be quite innocent and may be really good. Well let's shift the question a bit. A young man has been going with a young lady for a time and is sincerely fond of her and she of him. He gently and affectionately kisses her goodnight. A sin?"

She hesitates, but only because she is afraid she may be wrong in giving the answer she feels sure is right. "Why, I don't think so, father."

"And you are probably right. Note however the words gently and affectionately. There may be a danger that he won't be content with being merely gentle and affectionate, but in itself that kiss need not be sinful. But suppose the young man kisses the girl violently and at considerable length. She feels herself growing excited. She realizes that he has grown excited too. Is that a sin?"

I have never known a girl who failed to answer that question correctly. Usually she will say, simply:

"Yes; I see, father."

"What then makes the difference between a kiss that is guiltless and a kiss that becomes a sin or the occasion of sin? It's passion. And passion is one of those easily recognized things. When it is present in oneself, one feels it immediately. One clearly perceives its presence in someone else.

"So a kiss without passion may be a danger. If one is highly inflammable oneself or knows that the young man is inflammable, a kiss may be an occasion of sin. Sometimes it is the proximate occasion of sin. Difference of temperament enters into the case at this point. But it is almost impossible for young people, whom nature has made quite inflammable, to indulge in violent kissing or kissing for any length of time without having passion enter in. And once passion has entered . . . "

The girl has really explained her own case. She has given

the right answers. Those answers are satisfactory, whereas the counselor's categoric "Yes; kissing is sinful" or "No; kissing is not sinful" is not only unsatisfactory but is in each case incorrect.

The same line of questioning may be followed with the rather rare boy who asks a similar question about kissing. Most boys are quick to feel the element of passion in so far as it makes what started out to be an innocent kiss something not so innocent. They have less doubt about innocence or evil in a kiss than have girls. Their own quickly aroused passions act as a reliable barometer.

When Girls Ask

When girls come, as they will come, to ask for sex information from the priest or the religious who has been appointed their counselor, the course that can be followed is this:

First, we can advise them to ask for information and guidance from their parents.

I sincerely wish that that was the complete answer. The fact is that in ninety-nine cases out of a hundred, and possibly in the hundredth, the girl will reply: "I shouldn't dare to ask my mother such a question." And indeed she wouldn't. It is simply terrifying to realize how wide is the chasm between girls and their mothers on these matters. Girls do not ask their logical teachers—their parents. And their logical teachers shy away and almost run if the questions are asked.

So while I always give that as my first answer, I know that it is a formality and usually an entirely wasted gesture.

The second step is to measure as well as one can the questioner's age, experience, and reason for wanting to know. If the girl presents the question to a woman, whether a nun or a lay woman, the whole thing should be rather simple. But priests must be extremely careful not to barge in through an excess of honesty or plain speaking; they must be careful not to bruise sensitive feelings or unduly shock innocent souls.

There is a considerable difference in the extent of the information needed by different classes of girls. A young woman about to be married has a right to know all about the subject. It is little short of criminal to send her into marriage without telling her about the meaning of marriage. And her mother is the logical person to instruct her. The family doctor—if in this day of the impersonal specialist there is a family doctor and if he is a Catholic—is an acceptable person to do the explaining.

But the one in whom the young woman has trust, the one to whom she comes because she feels that he or she will give the desired information tactfully and unoffendingly is by reason of that trust constituted the proper informant.

Very young people, who are still far from marriage, should be given much less complete detail. It is sometimes surprising how little detail they really want and how well satisfied they are when the general relationships and principles are given them.

A tactless person should counsel youth in nothing. A person that is counseling youth in matters of purity must have more than tact; he must be extremely sensitive to attitudes, so sensitive that he feels the vibrations of innocence—that must not be jolted—or of guilelessness—that must not be shocked.

Measuring the needs and the reactions of the young person, the counselor asks her quite simply whether or not she really wants the truth. If the girl replies that she does (and likely enough she will say she does not, and the matter will end), the third step is called for.

Without hush or mystery the girl should be given the ideals of and the motives for purity. The connection between love and marriage and sex as we have already discussed it can be presented quite clearly. Much emphasis should be placed on the dignity of the creative act and the importance of love as a prelude to this act. The girl's own body should be spoken of as a beautiful and sacred thing, and it should be pointed out that the more completely feminine she is, the more beautiful and sacred will her body become.

Then, through a brief presentation of the facts of her own adolescence as she has experienced them, the essential difference between men and women can be shown quite simply and without unnecessary elaboration. The classic statues give the essential details of the difference between man's and woman's anatomy. She has already noticed this difference and to some extent accounted for it.

To no one except to a young woman ready for marriage need any of the details of the marital embrace be explained. But I should not hesitate to put it, as Father Bruckner equivalently does in his book "How to Give Sex Instruction," in frank but general terms even to youngsters: "Love is the desire of two young people to be united as closely as possible. Love draws the man and woman together so that out of their union will come a third life. Love is expressed in a close and affectionate embrace. Out of that embrace comes the perfect union of married life. And from it in some cases comes the beginning of the life of a little child."

I feel that those who have to give sex instruction should be almost rehearsed in what they mean to say and how they mean to say it. Bungling is fatal. Stumbling and speaking with an abashed air simply sets all nerves on edge. The counselor who will have to answer questions about sex again and again will do well to think out his approach carefully, to decide the very form of the words he means to use, to study carefully the psychological reactions of young people as he talks, and to keep constantly before his own eyes the constructive and positive side of purity.

One never shocks or harms by talking purity, even purity in its essential connection with the marital act. On that approach we are sound and safe.

THE BOY ASKS

Boys have the same quite normal curiosity that girls have, but they have it in a more exaggerated form. They are much more interested as a rule, and they do far more speculating.

When a boy presents his question, he can be answered in a straightforward, matter-of-fact fashion. He has asked an honest question, and he wants an honest answer. That is just what he rates and what he expects, otherwise he would not have come with his perplexity.

My own approach with boys (and often with girls) is to take them back to the moment when they themselves were born. I have discussed this at length in "The Pure of Heart," but to repeat briefly, this is what I do: I tell them of the great moment when their own father entered the darkened room where their mother lay with the tiny bit of life in her arms. I emphasize the trinity that is the father, the mother, and the baby; the joy the mother and father felt in their baby; the fullness of their love that was reached only when their love had blossomed in this child, who is now my questioner.

The steps from that point on are relatively simple. And neither boy nor girl feels any real embarrassment when the counselor talks in this fashion.

SOLITARY SIN

Solitary sin is the great peril of youngsters. With girls it is gratifyingly rare. With boys it is a hurdle that they have to take between the years of twelve and nineteen. Rare

is the lad who does not have that temptation; splendid is
the lad who constantly resists it.

Often it will happen that the boy contracts the habit
before he has the slightest idea that what he is doing is
wrong. No matter how the sin started, the youngster feels
a mortifying shame and comes to discuss his problem with
the greatest possible reluctance. Often enough he will regard
himself as utterly unnatural and abnormal. He will attribute
his temptation to all sorts of things: to the sins of his forebears, sins for which he is being punished; to some physical
defect; to some form of insanity.

Now there was a time when the method of handling young
people that were guilty of solitary sin was to tell them that
they were going to suffer frightful physical consequences because of it. This solitary sin would undermine their health; it
would make them physical weaklings; diseases would result.
As a consequence youngsters got into frightful states over it.
When night losses continued, as naturally and inevitably
happens in the case of all normal, unmarried males, they
wrongly thought that these were physically bad for them and
were the evil consequences of their sins.

It is the greatest possible mistake to tell youngsters that
solitary sin has physical consequences. If there are any ill
consequences, they are not the results of the sin but of the
mental worry and confusion that usually accompany it.
Nervousness may follow. Shame may bring about unfortu-
nate mental states. But there is no direct physical consequence worth bothering about, and it is wrong and unjust to
terrify youngsters with what will not happen.

In handling this problem the first approach is, as always,
purity in its positive and constructive aspect. If the boy or
girl has developed a deep respect for the creative act, he
will realize that solitary sin is a squandering of that act
and a betrayal of a sacred trust.

Then it is wise to show the youngster that this is an adolescent temptation which with advancing years will in all probability almost completely disappear. I do not hesitate to put it in this way:

"Yours is a temptation quite common in young people. Most boys (and a good many girls) experience this temptation between the ages of twelve and nineteen. All that this means is that you are growing up. You are developing the powers which will make you capable of being a father (or a mother). You have a new responsibility, and hence you are likely to be tempted to abuse that responsibility.

"But don't let that worry you. It is a temptation that grows steadily less strong. And in a short time it will disappear almost entirely. If you keep yourself pure now in the face of temptation, that particular temptation will eventually vanish, and you'll be a strong, well controlled, highly disciplined person."

While it is important to emphasize the supernatural remedies—Holy Communion received with frequency, ejaculatory prayer, devotion to the Blessed Virgin and to St. Aloysius—it is extremely wise to stress the natural remedies too. Boys and girls are tempted to solitary sin when they are idle or ill. The important counteraction against temptation is a busy mind in an energetic body. I put the case thus:

"You know by this time just when and where the temptation is likely to come to you. You can recognize the approach. Well when you feel that approach, don't start thinking about it and worrying about it. Don't even grit your teeth and say prayers violently. Those things may do no more than concentrate your attention on the temptation. You see, if you think of a sore toe too much, the toe hurts like the mischief. Keep your mind off your toe, and it won't hurt so much.

"So if you know that in a certain place you will be

tempted, and you have to go to that place, take a book along with you. Whistle or hum or sing out loud. Keep your mind busy and your thoughts cheerful. If the temptation comes upon you while you are alone, get up and turn on the radio. Call up a friend and talk to him. Go out and toss a ball around. Take a walk. Find somebody with whom you can chat. Do anything to keep yourself occupied. And the temptation will disappear."

I advise youngsters to read when they are in bed or in the bathroom. And the more exciting the reading, the better distraction it is from temptation.

It is wise too to show them the connection between impure thoughts and solitary sin. The impure thought is a prelude to the impure act. The pure mind insures the pure body. The impure mind insures the tempted and tortured body.

On the other hand young people should not be allowed to have exaggerated ideas about impurity of thought. They should be made to understand that here again temptation is merely a sign of developing maturity and the growth of those powers that are connected with parenthood. Temptation in itself is a natural thing. It is part of that attraction between the male and the female which is the basis of marriage and love. An evil thought or phantasm passing through the mind is an indication of growth. In itself it is no more sinful than a sneeze or an itch. It becomes sinful only when the person deliberately turns toward it, likes it, wants it, dwells on it with morbid or evil interest, or hugs it to his heart in secret desire.

Somewhere along the line counselors and guides of youth should give a simple, honest talk on impure thoughts, telling what they are not and what makes them sinful. The youngster feels highly reassured when he realizes that the fact of strange pictures flowing through his mind does not make him a pervert. He is consoled to know that these thoughts are really indications of his adult life. He feels normal again when he learns that attraction for those of the other sex is a natural thing, though a thing which has to be very carefully controlled. And he breathes a sigh of relief when he knows that only by an act of the will, a deliberate and fully conscious turning toward the evil thing in his mind, does he become guilty of sin.

On the other hand the wise director points out that while mental temptations are the fate of almost all human beings, only the fool deliberately looks for them. We have plenty of temptations rising from within; we need not go out looking for trouble. So the boy or girl who reads indecent books or looks at evil pictures or magazines, the boy or girl who through careless conduct or immodesty lets down the barriers of decency, who listens to or tells evil stories is merely piling up fuel for the fire of passion. He need not be surprised if he has plenty of problems, problems beyond those that nature normally gives young people. Nature's temptations will die down with time. But he can encourage an endless flow of temptation if he does not guard carefully what he reads, sees, hears, speaks, to what he is attracted by curiosity and interest.

The Difference Between Them

The guide and counselor of youth will somewhere along the line, either in group conferences or in personal talks, make clear the psychological differences between a man and a woman. A boy should understand that women are interested in affection and are comparatively free from passion. He should be made to see clearly that he wrongs a girl when he initiates her into the ways of passion, ways which she would not have learned without his tutelage. He must be made to understand how guilty is that man who imparts his own passionate temptations to a girl by awakening her to an evil which as a general rule does not easily touch a girl's nature.

On the other hand girls should know that men are far more passionate than are girls. Girls read into a man's conduct their own quite innocent desire for affection. Girls do not, unless they are told about it or run into it through unpleasant experience, realize how quickly man's passions flare and how violent are his desires. I do not hesitate to make this quite clear to girls:

"Man is the father; he is the aggressor. In a way he is the positive element in the marital relationship. Nature, or God through nature, has given him the stronger urge toward passion and its physical manifestation. He is easily tempted. He suffers much more from temptation than does a girl. He is more inclined to evil and to sin. You are more inclined to love, to affection; he is more inclined to passion, to violence. You are the stronger, because you are the less tempted. He is the weaker, because he is so violently tempted. He is quicker to take fire, because his passions are so vigorous. You are slower, because your passions are relatively weak.

"That is why you, the girl, must take care of the young man with whom you go out. You can, for you are less tempted than he is. His fate is more in your hands than you know. For passion tempts him to sin. And your affection and calmness should hold you back from sin and, holding you back, should hold him back too. Woman has always been the guardian of morality and of the world's goodness because she is less tempted, less violent in her desires, less explosive. And she must by her sweetness and affection and purity keep safe the young man who has not her natural self-restraint and relative freedom from temptation."

Girls understand that readily, and it does make a difference in their attitude toward the young men with whom they associate.

COMPANY KEEPING

If young people associate together freely and happily in crowds, they are less likely to be wandering off in twosomes. Recalling my own youth, I remember how the grand crowd with whom I was associated kept me so busy and contented that I preferred to be with the many rather than with any one. A wide social life prevents too early concentration on one boy or one girl.

Any boy or girl in the early or middle teens who thinks in terms of company-keeping should be treated with a bit of gentle ridicule. But ridicule is not quite enough. Parents who allow their children to start anything approaching steady company-keeping are just stupid. And schools that allow that sort of thing to become a practice are failing in their duty of guarding and guiding young people.

Putting the matter quite frankly to the young people themselves, one can indicate:

1. That by steady company-keeping at an early age they are missing very much. They miss the broadening of interests and sympathies that comes through contact with groups of young people. They cut themselves off from others. Normal, sane boys and girls fight shy of a couple that are "going steady" (to use the horrible words that are beaten only by the English phrase of the servant class, "walking out with"). The company-keepers think in terms of the interests and desires of one person, when they should be thinking of the teams they play on, the gang they run around with, the club they will join, the broad associations they should be establishing.

2. Company-keepers get themselves into real social jams. Very young people cannot concentrate on only one person without the probability of having their temptations increase. The girl is "taken off the market," and she misses the good times she could get in the less constrained and certainly less

emotionally taut society of a variety of young men. Boys are cut away from the other fellows by this concentration on one girl. Girls come to be out of sympathy with girls their own age.

3. Company-keeping cuts the period of their youth considerably. Steady keeping of company is meant only for those who are in a position seriously to think of marriage. For anyone else it is a waste of time and energy. They have to act older than their years, and later on the girl sincerely regrets it. "Oh, she went steady with so-and-so five years ago; that proves she's not as young as she pretends to be." "He's older than he likes to act. He was going steady with what's-her-name seven years ago." And undoubtedly the constant association with one person hastens the normal development of adolescence. Youngsters who start company-keeping too early come to have adult viewpoints and sometimes too early physical developments.

4. Seldom indeed does it happen that boys marry the sweethearts of their youth. In story books the hero returns to marry the girl he loved when she was in pigtails. But note that that is in story books, and that the hero returns. He does not stay on and continue to go with the girl up till the time he marries her. He leaves and then comes back. The intense excitement which sixteen feels for fifteen fades by seventeen or is superseded by an equally intense excitement over someone entirely different. How utterly immature and inexperienced are those youngsters in their teens who see in the first or second love the last and final love. And how stupid we elders are when we take these youngsters seriously or allow them to take themselves seriously.

Youthful social life, which should mean seeing a great deal of a great many people, is the best way to prevent concentration on one person. Time enough for the concentration when the boy has a job that makes marriage more than a mirage.

Going Together

If the young man and the young woman have been thoroughly grounded in the constructive, positive ideals of purity, their going together may be fairly safe and entirely wholesome. The young man will see in the girl toward whom he is attracted the potential mother of children, possibly his own. The young woman will take care of the young man, for she will realize that he may possibly be the man she will marry. They will safeguard themselves; they will be sane enough to safeguard each other.

Mutual respect while going together is one of the surest guarantees of a happy marriage. The couple that do not respect themselves before marriage are entering marriage with low ideals, and they will certainly have little or no respect for each other when they are torn by the trials and difficulties of the married state.

Young people should be made to see (and we can put it before them quite clearly):

1. That the man who asks improper liberties of a girl before marriage may do so because he desires her fiercely, but he does not love her well enough to protect her against the animal in his own nature.

2. That the girl who allows improper liberties before marriage sees the sexual relationship, not as something to be consecrated by a sacrament, but as something to be reduced to the level of entirely selfish enjoyment.

3. That God is not likely to bless the marriage which is entered upon only after the man and the woman have misused the sacred powers which marriage consecrates to high purposes.

4. That the first use of the sexual act is an extremely important one; that it brings about definite physical changes in the woman; that it arouses tremendous, one might almost say convulsing, changes in the psychology of both the man and the woman; hence, far from being a light and casual thing, it is an extremely fundamental thing, the results of which are far-reaching.

5. That the man who cannot stay pure before marriage, who cannot hold his passionate nature in restraint, may well be regarded after marriage with suspicion; the wife knows he could not exercise self-control before marriage, and that might be accepted as more than a fair guarantee of his inability to resist temptation after marriage.

6. That the woman who is not strong enough to say no to the man she loves when she knows that her consent will do him harm is not likely to say no to some other attractive man later. It is a well known fact that impurity before marriage is an indication of probable infidelity after marriage.

Men and women who enter marriage after carelessness before marriage are notoriously suspicious of one another. They remember their former falls. They suspect that their partner in marriage may fall again. For if one has little respect before marriage for the great creative power, what guarantee is there that a sudden respect will develop after marriage? The cynical worldling knows quite as well as does the sincere Catholic the truth of this recurrent human experience: Impure before, unfaithful after.

So many a marriage is wrecked by sexual carelessness before ever the marriage is made. Seeds of suspicion are sown. The edge of complete happiness is taken off the marital relationship. The remembered past brings regrets and breeds doubts. The argument that lurks in the back of troubled minds is: "He or she fell before. Will that happen again?"

Neither Too Long nor Too Short

Hence counselors and guides of youth are wise to indicate that courtships should not be too short or too long.

Courtships should be long enough to permit each to see the other's faults and virtues quite thoroughly, to learn each other's interests, likes, family, backgrounds, limitations, habits, and manner of work and of play.

Courtships should be short enough to ward off those things which make courtship a problem and a danger and marriage a bore. Two young people cannot love each other well enough for marriage without feeling a strong physical urge. If they continue to go together over a prolonged period of years, passion and the mutual physical attraction will grow frightfully strong. The strength of these things will make both of them nervous, irritable, quick to quarrel, eager to see each other yet restless in each other's company. The man will grow petulant. The girl will find his manner offensive. They will begin to punctuate their association with spats, with situations that they feel are dangerous, with an alternation of passionate attraction toward and instinctive or cultivated drawing away from one another. And in the end the man without notice often switches to some other girl, whom he eventually marries. The first girl, now well past the period of her highest charms, is deprived of much of her hope for a successful marriage.

Or after the long years of waiting, they marry. Marriage has lost its appeal. They know each other too well. They have seen too much of each other. For a long time they had been married without being married, tied to each other without any visible bonds. Marriage has been staled before the actual marriage. They face the real marriage with developed ennui.

I feel it is important to instruct young people early not to think of marriage until they can see it fairly close on the horizon. Elopements and quick marriages, the Church knows, are nearly always fatal. That is why the Church demands that the banns be read on at least three successive Sundays. But marriages long delayed often do not come off at all. And when they do, they are entered upon by jaded people who have lost their zest and see only weariness ahead.

QUALITIES

Young people often ask their advisers what qualities they should seek in their future partners. I have discussed that at considerable length elsewhere. In spite of the old saying that opposites attract and that unlike traits of character blend in a satisfactory marriage, the counselor would still do well to suggest that young people demand that their future partner be like themselves at least in these points:

1. They should be alike in religious belief. This is essential. Without it the chance for a happy marriage is nowadays about one in fifty.

2. They should have similar backgrounds, to this extent at least: that they will be willing to get along in the same sphere of life. If she is accustomed to Rolls-Royces and he to Fords, there may be difficulty in adjusting her standards to his. If he is college-bred and she did not finish the sixth grade, even though the passionate attraction between them is strong, their separate outlooks are much too different for happiness; their trainings have split them too widely apart.

3. They should be alike in some of their major interests. Passion as an interest will not be enough. Prettiness fades; physical charm diminishes. If both want children or if both are interested in building a home; if he finds her sympathetic toward his career and profession or if he is interested in her friends and hobbies; if they can talk books or the theater or music or science together; if each has sufficient breadth of developed interest to be glad when the other has

interests, even if those interests are not mutually shared—in all those cases the chances for success in marriage are heightened.

But keep repeating to the young people who consult you: "Passion is not enough. Physical attraction which is no more than physical attraction fades and leaves marriage barren and hollow. Passion is important, since man is a creature composed of body and soul. There should be an element of physical attraction. But if that is all there is, it is not sufficient. It fades and becomes empty unless it is buttressed with other interests that knit the mind and soul as well as the body."

May I remind counselors that it is too late to present wise saws and convincing maxims after the young man or young woman has actually fallen in love? Our job is to create a state of mind about marriage. Our sane views, which must be of course the views of wise old mother Church, should early be ingrained in the young people. Reading will help establish those views, and fortunately there are excellent books and booklets that we can give our young people. Our talks to groups should cover sound Catholic principles for married life. The creation of a right attitude will prevent the duchess's falling in love with the coachman and the Catholic's falling in love with a person that is blind to all the beauty and truth of the faith.

Our task is not so much the guidance of the young person after he has been obsessed with that thing called love; it is the guidance of that young person long before he has been obsessed. Advice won't affect the obsessed. Even exorcism will do little to help them. But I have noticed how often children are saved from stupid marriages, not by any logical reasoning at the time of passionate attraction, but by a previously laid foundation of good sense. They were convinced that a Catholic marriage to an atheist, no matter how attractive the atheist might be, was doomed to misery. They saw that wide divergence in education might be an insurmountable barrier to happiness in marriage. They might be drawn powerfully by physical attraction, but they were instinctively convinced that there must be more than the physical to the making of a successful marriage. Their inbred respect for marriage as the sacrament of the future gave them clear vision at a time when the hot mist of passion would have blinded the less well prepared.

It is too late to instruct and exhort and threaten one when he is deep in love. All instruction and exhortation must be given in the years of adolescence, for then the minds of youth are impressionable, and upon them we can engrave standards and ideals and principles strong enough to enable youth to resist folly, no matter how attractive a form that folly assumes.

GUIDING THE FUTURE

A terrifying number of young people simply stumble into life.

They leave school with the general preparation given them in the classroom, in the home, and in the Church, and they fall blindly into the first job that comes their way.

Years later they wonder why they are so discontented. They look back over the bleak mediocrity of their lives. They see others who went ahead while they stood still or retrogressed into depressed, dull-grey middle age, and they can't see just where they themselves missed out.

"I should have been a priest," says the gray-haired man who has always just missed out in everything he did. The truth of the matter is, he should have been a priest. "I stumbled into law because all my associates thought that was a wonderful profession for a young man; I probably would have made a good automobile mechanic," says the disgruntled lawyer. And as an automobile mechanic he would have led a brisk, energetic, satisfying out-of-door life.

"I became a teacher because my parents thought it was a safe job with a sure future," sighs the woman who in her younger days was aboundingly attractive. "I was never meant to be a teacher, and following the profession unfitted me for marriage. Marriage, I know now, is what I wanted." "I drifted into a department store, and here I am, still behind the counter." "I should have been a newspaperwoman." "I had a great gift for music." . . .

If the saddest of all sad words are uttered by the might-have-beens, we guides of youth are responsible for much sad speech. Young people cannot be allowed to drift. It is our job to direct those young people.

I have no intention of attempting in this slender book to give extensive time to this wide subject of career and guidance in vocation. I have treated the subject more at length in a booklet titled "How to Pick a Successful Career." Fortunately vocational guidance is becoming an almost exact science, and its literature grows increasingly intelligent, helpful, and accessible. In this book I can call attention to only a few fundamental things.

The first of these fundamentals I have already stated: We have the obligation of watching our young people and helping them to utilize their talents and abilities in the careers for which they are best suited.

This obligation we can begin to fulfill by giving general talks on vocation. Vocation for many a priest and religious has meant simply the priestly or religious vocation. Now the priest or religious should certainly give a fair and outspoken statement in favor of the vocation in which he himself has found personal happiness. Young people expect that. They want it. They have on occasion loudly complained to me that "I went through a Catholic school for four years and never heard one word about the priesthood or the religious life." Incredible but true. To take aside one or two chosen souls with the kindly intention of babying their vocation into some semblance of sturdy maturity is by no means to fulfill sufficiently the counselor's obligation. Some young people that seem to have the priestly or religious vocation written all over them often really have no such vocation. And a boy or a girl that is just waiting for someone to suggest the higher life may be sitting at his desk, completely neglected. When no one does suggest the religious vocation and no one bothers to discuss it in chapel when he is there, he gives up the idea.

It just happens that I was practically the only young man in my graduating class to whom the dean did not give a booklet about the religious life. The dean concentrated on one young fellow who was notably pious, which I certainly was not. But one young scholastic thought there were possibilities even in my frankly pleasure-loving nature, and he broached the subject. The dean thought the scholastic a little mad. I finished college and went to the novitiate the following month. The young fellow on whom the dean had been concentrating married the girl he had taken to the senior dance. You can never tell.

But the guide and counselor has an obligation beyond that of giving priestly and religious vocation talks; he has the obligation of acting as director in other fields as well. Hence the importance of general talks on vocations: What fits men and women for certain careers; what certain careers offer by way of opportunity; what careers are crowded and what sort of equipment is needed to rise above the crowds; what careers are inviting at the present moment; what careers require exceptional skill, etc.

In order to supplement his own talks in these matters,

the guide can well bring in to meet his young people men and women who are successful in various careers. If these men and women can give a good talk, let them. If they don't want to give a talk, ask them to come and let the young people put questions to them. Any man or woman who is doing well in a profession can certainly answer questions about the profession. The word of an expert is, naturally enough, the word that the person contemplating life anxiously awaits and gratefully hears.

General talks will satisfy the general crowd. But the guide owes his young people more than that. The teacher in the classroom soon comes to know a great deal about the outstanding characteristics of his students. The priest who works alertly with youngsters comes to estimate with considerable accuracy what they do well and what they do badly.

This knowledge makes the counselor an excellent judge to whom the young man or young woman facing the future can present his case. The analysis of individual characteristics is the one basis on which can be established any sort of estimate of a person's chance for future success. This analysis must of course be measured against the status of the various fields of human endeavor as they are right here and now and as they probably will be if the world continues in its present direction.

Time and thought will be needed to appraise the young person's abilities. He rates that time and thought, and, if we are real counselors, we will give him that time and thought. Especially will we keep our eyes open for those qualities which he possesses in an unique or extraordinary degree. These are the qualities that can, if properly exercised, take him out of the rut and lift him above mediocrity. They should be pointed out and measured with an eye to their suitability for the careers which are open and inviting today.

A little observation and consultation will bring the counselor the information he needs about these modern careers. Law may be crowded; social law is not, and international law is an almost uncultivated field. There may be too many doctors; there are not too many doctors who are doing research. The trend toward social legislation is opening unlimited careers for young men and women. The awakening of our people to the corrupt spoils system and our tendency to admire the English civil servant will make for careers in government, careers that will not depend upon the caprices of elections. Radio is now overcrowded as a field; television has not as yet claimed its quota of engineers and entertainers. The theater is fading out, and the motion pictures are jammed to suffocation with eager if starving souls; the lecture platform is never jammed; only Ruth Draper, Cornelia Otis Skinner, and Dorothy Sands are today outstanding in the field of the monologue entertainment, and no man has taken his place with them.

Newspapers can buy their writers for fifteen cents a dozen; magazines are clamoring for the smart young man or woman with a certain degree of talent who is willing to learn the technique of successful fiction writing.

And so it goes. The counselor and guide of youth must measure the abilities of the young people who consult him. He must place these abilities against the careers available today. He must point out openings that have not been noticed and that wait to be filled. He must deflect his consultants from the overcrowded, the monotonous, the hopeless jobs to the jobs where those consultants can earn a decent living, share a life that has something of the creative about it, and enjoy a reasonable security. If a young person has active hands, it may be wrong to let him drift into a profession that requires a brilliant head. If the creative arts are impatient of any except superlative ability, the mechanical arts are quite willing to be served by a degree of earnestness that perhaps masks less than ordinary cleverness.

Ours is the pleasant task of putting round pegs into round holes and square pegs into square holes.

Which is just another way of saying that our counsel and advice may make the difference between a success and a failure, a man happy in a full life or one struggling against the oppressive feeling of unfitness for his life's task.

THE RELIGIOUS "SIDE"

There is no such thing as the religious "side" to anything we Catholic guides and counselors do. I have been more and more astonished these last few years to notice youth programs that were divided, let's say, into the athletic side, the intellectual side, the artistic side, and the religious side. And thinking young people have been more astonished than I.

For Catholicism is not a "side"; it is a complete life. One cannot be an athlete from eight to ten o'clock, an intellectual man from ten to twelve, an artist from twelve to two, and a Catholic from two to four. That is inconceivable. A Catholic must be a Catholic in all that he does. His thought must be Catholic; his play must be Catholic; his achievements must be Catholic.

In this aspect of complete focus our enemies have shown us a pair of clean heels. The communist expects young people to be communists twenty-four hours a day. Communists would no more talk about a communistic side of their program than they would talk about the hours of the day during which they would be men. The communist believes that communism is a permeating thing, that a communist is a communist when he throws a ball or writes plays or sings songs or paints pictures or builds bridges or collects stamps or goes for a hike or attends class or eats his dinner.

The nazi and the fascist have much the same attitude.

A nazi's victories on the athletic field are triumphs for the one important cause. His paintings advance that cause. His songs and plays and games and study clubs and hobbies are propaganda. His beliefs are at work twenty-four hours a day.

We Catholics lived for many years in a land in which we were expected to sever our faith from our lives for long periods of time. We were Catholics, yes; but we were Catholics on a part-time basis. We saw our public schools completely divorced from God. When we went to the theater, we saw a non-Catholic or an anti-Catholic play, for it was almost impossible to find a Catholic play. The majority of the books we read and studied were pagan or Protestant and sometimes bitterly or cynically anti-Catholic. We had to soft-pedal our faith because so much of our life was spent with men and women who knew less of our faith than they knew of Shintoism. We dared not vote as Catholics. Religion was not given a warm welcome in our business relationships. Even our Catholic schools had to join standardizing agencies, which simply waived our classes in religion as trivial and not worth considering—if they did not make it almost impossible to telescope those classes into the schedules crowded with important things like science and literature and the date of Cæsar's crossing of the Rubicon.

I bow respectfully to the communists, the nazis, and the fascists, who have made belief once more a twenty-four-hour-a-day affair. My thanks to the men who have realized that if you are thoroughly convinced of a thing that thing goes with you everywhere you are and into everything you do.

May I suggest that young people have been a bit mystified when they have paused to think of the way in which religion has been given a poor third or fourth place even by those of us who are supposed to be religion's professional representatives? Our schools put religion first in the catalogue, but they put it first in no other place. Our parish dramatic clubs present stale Broadway plays of ancient vintage. Our Catholic authors easily stray into the folds of the secular publisher, where the grass is green and the royalties are large—but not for the writer who puts his religion into his writings. Catholic athletes adopt the low standards of the men who look upon the ancient Greek athlete as the embodiment of the highest athletic ideals. The Catholic businessman at communion breakfasts listens to speeches about the Papal encyclicals but never bothers to find out whether or not those encyclicals possibly have some relation to the way he runs his own business. Catholic politicians are the very engineers who in too, too many cases oil the wheels of the big political machines and give wise advice on the subject of that contradiction in terms, honest graft.

Youth finds this all very, very confusing. If Catholicity is the tremendous thing that we say it is, why is it that communism and fascism dominate all that young communists and fascists do and think, while Catholicism is often no more than a slight auxiliary factor in the life of Catholics? In fact the most common Catholic attitude toward the practice of Catholicism has been this: If a Catholic keeps the commandments, goes to Mass and the sacraments with fair regularity, and contributes to the support of his pastor, he is in the class of the better-type believer. He need not be too ostentatious about his faith in those places where things of importance happen—the office, the warehouse, the capitol, the legislature, the playing field, the theater, the press room, the army and navy.

No one ever dared teach that theory as a principle. But we have seen that theory alarmingly applied in practice. Only the Holy Father's insistent call to Catholic Action has saved religion from being compartmented, from being divorced from all the practical affairs of life. And young people have often swung to communism and fascism because communism and fascism regard watertight compartmenting of belief as treason to the cause.

There is no Catholic "side" to any program for Catholic youth. Catholicism must dominate all that our young people do and think. Religion must permeate the ideals, develop the plans, carry out the programs, dominate the whole of the young people's lives.

Mistaken Attitude Toward Youth

We have underestimated our young people. We have started by setting too low a standard for them.

I once heard a famous president of a Catholic university remark with forceful conviction: "If I keep my students out of bad houses and get them to Mass on Sunday and to the sacraments once a month, they'll be doing all that I can expect them to do."

The one major fault with his argument was simply this: If that was all he asked, he was not likely to get even that much. If he had asked for high heroism and daily communion, he might have got at least the lesser achievement.

Here again the enemy has put high the standards for its young people. It has trained them to heroism. Youth in Russia and Germany is made to believe that it was born to die for its country. Communism has asked young people to man the picket lines, to give their hands in friendship to the oppressed and depressed classes, to distribute literature wherever they go, to throw their whole enthusiasm into the creation and presentation of a propaganda art and literature, to give up all thought of the "profit motive" in order to dedicate themselves body and soul to the cause.

We ask all that of our priests and religious. We have not asked it of those equally fine and brave young men and women who carry on the work of the world.

Vincent Sheehan in his "Personal History" tells with enthusiasm of the young woman communist he met in his journeying; he saw her in Russia, in China, on a half-dozen battlefronts. He likens her to a flame, for she simply burned with enthusiasm for the cause. She darted like a flame, glowed like a flame, shone forth with the light of a flame, in the end died like a flame.

That's fine. But it was Christ who said to His followers: "So let your light shine before men, that they may see your good works, and glorify your Father who is in heaven." If men and women are to burn with zeal, they can burn with nothing that is even comparable to the love of God and their fellow men. If we have not the torch of truth, who in the world has?

The term flaming youth became a joke as the people to whom it applied became a nuisance. Yet youth wants to flame, and there is no other period of life to equal the enthusiasm and zeal with which youth catches on fire. If we don't set youth on fire with our zeal, the enemy will. Youth will glow with a light that is Catholic, or youth will glow with that smudgy flame that is communistic or nazi.

We must realize that among all our groups of young people there are potential heroes and martyrs. The spirit of sacrifice lies latent in most young hearts. Young people want to have their ideals lifted high. But many a guide and counselor of youth decides that these young people are selfish and hopeless and greedy and lazy; he lets slide the moments when he might be lifting them to Christian idealism, and he leaves their enthusiasms to be caught and enkindled by God's enemies. Or he sends out from his listless hands dull clods who will do nothing for God and little for the cause which is Christ's.

Remember: Every cause that is making headway in the world today is demanding frightful sacrifices of youth.

Youth must die at the barricades. Youth must work on starvation rations. Youth must throw in its labor with this five-year plan or that ten-year plan. Youth must follow a leader blindly. Youth must be killed if need be in order that the cause may advance.

The name Dorothy Day has become familiar to anyone who is dealing with young people. Whatever one may think of her or of her principles, this no one can deny: Dorothy Day can inspire a crowd of young people to reach for and carry through heroic and unpleasant things. She can say to them, "Don't ever think of making money," and they understand her. She can challenge them to go down and clean up a filthy hovel in the Negro quarter, and they are there with buckets and mops and their willing hands and sensitive knees. She can dare them to match the restless vigor of the communists, and they do it.

Dorothy Day is no genius. But she has the good common sense to realize that young people yawn at low ideals and are bored by the people who offer them nothing but the commonplace. A few more of us could safely give a little less attention to quarreling with Miss Day's specific program and a little more attention to profiting from the way in which she appeals to the unselfish idealism of young people.

If high standards are set for our young people, some of those young people will reach those standards. The majority, led on by those high standards, will rise to at least notable standards of mediocrity—which sounds like a contradiction, but isn't. If low standards are set, the majority will barely reach those standards. And where will the superior young people get their inspiration and their impulse toward real spiritual achievement?

I like to tell of the incident which happened in one of America's largest diocesan seminaries a number of years ago. Because this seminary had so many young men training for the priesthood, the superior encouraged each religious order to present the advantages of its life and work to the seminarians. If any of the seminarians cared to join one of these communities, they were free to do so. Representatives of various orders came, and most of them left with one or more applicants. One community's representative arrived and presented this plea: "You'll find ours a pleasant and happy life. We try to discover what you are best suited for, and we put you into that sort of work. We give you a splendid training, but we like you to select your own lifework. We sincerely try to make our members contented." Though the hard-working missionaries had gone away with applicants and even the rigorous contemplatives had taken a candidate, this congregation of the "easy life" got not a single nibble. Youth was not inspired by the inducement that they would have their inclinations consulted and that they would find a contented life.

That's youth, and that's a side of youth that we are prone to overlook.

SOFT PEDALING?

Counselors and guides of youth should be careful:

1. Never to soft-pedal the spiritual element of the Church in favor of the purely social or recreational element. That has become a tendency in certain circles. It's a mistake. We cannot possibly compete with the elaborate social and recreational programs offered to our young people today. The best parish hall cannot compare with the nearby Y. M. C. A. or with the neighborhood motion-picture palace. We are superlatively good only in the spiritual element. That element we betray when we push it aside for any program, however attractive, that is not basically spiritual and interestingly religious.

2. Never to belittle the spiritual element. Sometimes this

is done in words. Those in charge of youth have an occasional pitying smile for the good people whom they charac-
terize as zealots and fanatics. A great many saints were in
their own day often regarded by the casual observers as
zealots and fanatics. Young people do not like to have the
contemptuous word flung at anyone, not even the person who
carries religion to the point of annoyance. In fact they find
the so-called fanatic's attitude more logical than that of the
Catholic who takes his religion as something only a trifle
more important than an occasional chocolate soda.

It is not necessary to note unpleasantly that priests and
religious are sometimes quite frankly uninterested in the
spiritual element. Said a certain young lady to me: "We
used to have a hard time getting the director to come to our
Sodality meetings. But we found that we could always get
him if we had food, so we always have food." Said the best
student in a certain boys' high school: "I'm through trying
to do anything for Catholic Action. Not a member of the
faculty really gives a damn. I'm manager of the football
team, and I'm also the head of our students' spiritual organization. I put in three or four hours a night and most of
Saturday working with the team. But when I want to take
off two hours from the team on Saturday morning for a
meeting of the officers of our students' spiritual union, the
faculty throws a fit. They want a successful team, but they
don't give a rap whether or not we have a good spiritual
organization."

Here are verbatim comments made to me so often that
they are no longer novel: "Our school makes up a fifteen-
thousand-dollar deficit on athletics every year, but the ad-
ministration has a spasm if I ask for ten dollars for the
Sodality." . . . "The glee club was given money for a long
trip last year; but the school gives us no help toward send-
ing students to the spiritual convention or a Summer School

of Catholic Action." . . . "Our director will work like a dog
to put over a successful play; he doesn't even want to give
a talk at our spiritual meetings." . . . "That dean is so
busy talking to prospective athletes that he can't see any of
the ordinary kids." . . . "We spent five dollars each on a
dance; we can't collect ten cents a month for the missions;
but then the director wanted a successful dance." . . . "If
our society makes money for the parish, that's all the pastor
cares about." . . . "Our adviser is a clever person, but she'd
rather see the girls fashionable than social-minded."

The Adviser's Part

Certainly the adviser plays the most important part in
the creation of enthusiasm for Catholicity. What he or she
says is important. But what he or she does, how he or she
lives is essential.

The personal cheerfulness that the young people see in
the eyes of a priest or a religious is one of the strongest
arguments for religion's importance. The enthusiasm for and
love of the life he has chosen is the great proof of the sincerity of a religious. A wise old director once remarked that
in Jesuit schools the number of vocations to priestly and religious life was in exact ratio to the number of happy teaching
scholastics on the faculty. These young Jesuit scholastics
were close to the boys. When the boys saw that the scholastics loved their life and were intensely happy in it, no words
of argument were necessary. A happy life is a great demon-
stration. The habitual smile on the face of a priest or a
religious is a great argument for the beauty and happiness
of religion itself.

Young people watch their religious leaders with coldly
logical eyes. Sermons and talks are only mildly effective. It
is spirit and conduct that count. The priest and religious
who show a spirit of zeal for religion need hardly speak about
religion. Their actions are their most profound sermons. If

they are devoted to the young people entrusted to them, if they give them time and attention, if they are—assuming that they are priests—careful about their sermons and willing at all times to listen to confessions, if they work for the things they say are important, talk is merely a reenforcement. Their deeds speak and speak loudly and convincingly.

The director or guide cannot expect to arouse enthusiasm for religion unless he shows a personal love of souls. Behind his talks must lie action. If he gives a liturgical talk, he must be willing to take the time necesesary to train young people to participate in the liturgy. If he talks on prayer, he must realize that the talk is only prelude to the training that is necessary to teach the young people how to pray. If he talks charity, he must demonstrate charity by the universal attitude he takes toward his charges and by the broad charity that keeps all unkindness out of his personal attitudes. Exhortations to zeal are useless when they come from a man who is not personally zealous.

All of this simply stresses the obvious. Eloquence never fools the young. Actions are what count. Young people discount speech in the presence of attitudes that are unmistakably contradictory. They want a leader who, as St. Ignatius said of Christ, never orders us to go but always begs us to come; who doesn't exhort but leads; who so loves the things he preaches that he holds those things personally dear; who asks of others only those ideals and heroisms which he himself exemplifies in his life.

And that puts us guides and counselors in something of a demanding position. We should for a while stop blaming young people and should start examining our own consciences. If we put golf or biology or general cleverness before Christ's immediate interests, we cannot expect our young people to do otherwise. If we prefer a successful football team to a good Sodality, if we are more interested in a "bang-up" prom than in a splendid retreat, if we talk eloquently when the time comes for a collection and in sloppy fashion when we are handling a spiritual subject, if we exhort people to read Catholic books of which we are notably neglectful, if we preach zeal while we practice considerable selfishness, if we theorize about the value of individual souls or social justice or mental prayer while we are obviously interested in a few favorites or in the movies or in our personal convenience . . . well youth is logical and youth draws the inevitable conclusions.

Unity and Cooperation

Seldom does it happen that a person stands alone and in isolation when he is dealing with young people. The counselor is either a member of a school faculty or a priest in a parish. Always he is a part of the Church Universal.

Now one of the things that most puzzles young people is the disunion and the lack of cooperation they find among priests and religious. They are astounded when first they learn that diocesan priests and order priests are—shall we put it mildly?—sometimes not on the best of terms. They are pained when they learn of disunion within a religious community. They cannot understand why a Catholic leader should not have a Catholic viewpoint, why a Catholic leader should not realize that no Catholic success can be won without his own position being strengthened, why a Catholic leader should not know that a disaster that strikes an individual or a community or a country strikes, through the wounded member, the whole Mystical Body of Christ.

"I could never become a member of that religious community," confided a boy; "the priests just don't agree among themselves." "Go to their novitiate?" exclaimed a girl who was speaking of the order that had taught her. "Never! Why they get along like cats." "He's the only man on the faculty that is really interested in the boys," said another youth, "and the rest of the faculty act as if he were a little queer." "The young priest in our parish doesn't have a chance," said the president of the parish society. "The pastor is jealous of any priest that does well. So the assistant has to take things quietly." "I'd like to invite you to come to our town," more than one honest if slightly abashed soul has said, "but you know our director doesn't like Jesuits." Or, changing that slightly: "I was so shocked when I found out that there were priests who don't like Jesuits."

A smart director of young people should, just in the interests of his own good name if for no higher motive, adopt the fixed principle never under any circumstances to belittle any man's sincere and honest work. Such a director, who speaks well of the work of all his colleagues, is the honored member of a faculty. The priest who is ready to place young people under the ministrations of any other priest they may happen to like is the priest that draws young people to himself. That man who cheers, and cheers sincerely, for the successful work done by anyone for Christ and His Church is the man that is advancing his own work.

Believe me, young people are logical and relentless critics. And believe me again, we give them much too much opportunity for saying that we dislike one another and are hopelessly divided.

The competent director will show, not in words, but in actions, a complete willingness to cooperate with his associates. He will be frankly glad of their good deeds, frankly happy in the friendships they make. A transparent friendliness and charity running through a faculty or a parish house is not merely Catholic in spirit but Catholic in effect. It draws young people by that same motive that drew the early pagans: "See these Christians, how they love one another."

The director or counselor or guide has handicapped himself (and just as much herself) when he lets dislike for other directors or counselors or guides appear in his attitude toward them. Jealousy paralyzes young people. Disunity terrifies them. Contempt for any fellow priest or religious or envy of his achievements hurts only the one who feels it. And it hurts him most of all in the eyes of those who expect to find in their counselors patterns of the outstanding Christian virtues—"and the greatest of these is charity."

Fundamental Approach to the Spiritual

Too long has religion been treated as a conservative thing. Religion is a revolution.

I shall not take time to discuss this again. I have treated it elsewhere, but in so doing I have done no more than echo the universal attitude of the Apostles and the missionaries and the martyrs and the doctors and the confessors and the great Catholic men and Catholic women who have as members of the Church Militant ever carried forward the interests of Christ's kingdom.

The Church Militant! There's a phrase that appeals to youth. Not the Church dormant or the Church snoozing or the Church apathetic, but the Church advancing in battle array to the conquest of the world for Christ!

It is perfectly true that the Church does conserve. She conserved the classic languages and literatures. She struggles to conserve the great works of art against the Russian bombers and the Red dynamiters of Spain. She believes that man is safe only when she conserves those things that make for his dignity, that safeguard his interests, that uphold the moral law — that law which expresses the only sane and decent way in which men can deal with one another.

But religion is first of all a revolution. Then it is an endless warfare, not of defense, but of glorious aggression.

And modern youth is in a fair way of missing all that. We have allowed ourselves to be shoved into the camp of the listless conservatives, the worshipers of things-as-they-are. Youth doesn't like that. And I for one certainly do not blame them.

Priests and religious have time and again been told the story of St. Ignatius and St. Francis Xavier. They hear how this brilliant young university professor and athlete, Xavier, is haunted by the gaunt figure of Ignatius, who over and over again repeats: "Xavier, what doth it profit a man to gain the whole world and suffer the loss of his own soul?" In the end, they are told, Ignatius won. Xavier yielded. He decided to save his soul.

Now if that were really the end of the story—and it is usually the point at which the story is stopped—the tale would be doleful enough. This brilliant flame that is Xavier is quenched in a downpour of words. The brilliant light that might have flamed across Europe is dimmed to a votive candle. Xavier retires to a novitiate.

But that is far from being the whole story. That is only the beginning. Xavier took Ignatius's phrase and gave it real meaning. He saved his soul; no doubt of that. But in saving his soul he gained a world. He plunged out and conquered half a continent. And even had he retired into a cloister, he might—as did Theresa of Avila—have conquered the world. As it was, his flame became the light of Asia. His restless energy was not quenched; it was merely diverted into gloriously constructive channels. Instead of becoming a professor and wrestling with syllogisms and digging up word-roots, he became a soldier who carried the cross of Christ in conquest across a world.

The really significant thing which Ignatius said to Xavier is the thing that our conservative tellers of tales never repeat. Ignatius turned to this man he had won for God and cried out: "Go, and set the world on fire for Christ!" Xavier did, and in setting the world on fire he saved his immortal soul and rose to the heights of sanctity.

There is a tendency to say to young people, "Be careful," when we should be saying, "Be reckless." We say, "Alas, the world is full of revolutionists!" when we should be saying, "How dare we let these fake revolutionists work so hard? We, the real revolutionists, should be winning mankind and completely revolutionizing the world for Christ." We are allowing ourselves to be listed as conservatives when we are of that band of glorious revolutionists that spring from the revolutionary Christ and the world-conquering Paul, when we are one with the men and women who died to overturn paganism, one with Francis, who upset all the false ideas of values, with Bernard and Dominic and Hildebrand, with the Little Flower—all leaders of a revolution in world ideas, all revolutionists who take the heart of God by storm and lay siege to the heart of the world.

I am not now going to discuss the revolutionary character of the spirituality we preach. But baptism is a revolution, the overthrow of the kingdom of evil and the establishment of the kingdom of Christ. Every confession of mortal sin is a revolution. Every time a man gives himself unreservedly to the service of Christ he has conducted a successful revolution.

No one who accepts the principles of Christ can be other than a divinely discontented revolutionary. Christ always talked in terms of advancing the kingdom of God. And that kingdom will be established only when the hideous kingdom of injustice and evil has been overthrown. That is why the Roman emperors hated Christianity; they cared nothing for any of its doctrine; but they feared its revolutionary doctrine that declared that men were equal and that tyrants must be overthrown. That doctrine has frightened tyrants

from the days of Nero to our days of Stalin and Hitler.
Tyrants cannot tolerate the revolutionary doctrine that the
individual man is precious in God's sight and that tyrants
who play with life and death will stand as criminals before
God's judgment seat.

Once one has accepted the doctrine of the Mystical Body,
revolution follows. Class warfare and the disunion of races
and the color line and human hatreds must go. Brotherhood,
about which people theorize and which they dare not practice, must follow. All the social implications of Christianity,
far-reaching beyond the widest sweep of man's imagination,
imply revolutionary stands and revolutionary advances.

And this is what we should be showing to our young
people—those young people who are on the side of the radicals, those radicals who go down to the roots of things, yes,
even to that root which is the divine branch, onto which all
mankind is grafted. Young people are as radical as the
Sacred Heart of Christ, that beats in the hope of overturning evil wherever it is established. They are not with
the pale conservatives, struggling to keep things as they
are; they are with Christ, who marched with knotted whips
through a profaned temple, who preached from the Mount
truths so world-convulsing that their mere utterance shakes
men to their deepest souls, who fought on Calvary the life-
and-death struggle with the devil and his powers and flung
them down in defeat together with disloyal Judea and cynical Rome.

When we begin to show young people religion as it is—
a terrific struggle to bring about that world revolution which
is the establishment of the kingdom of Jesus Christ—we can
expect the young people to flame with enthusiasm. But they
are not going to be enthusiastic about a spiritual policeman
that stands guard over things as they are and protects

vested interests which had better not be too carefully examined.

We guides and counselors of youth are really professors training young people to set the world on fire with the love of Christ. Certainly that task permits no pale and anemic attitude toward the religion we teach or the spirituality with which we must permeate our youth.

GUARDIAN OF RIGHTS

The Church Militant is the Church which we must more and more preach and talk today. Although our enemies have boasted that they are fighting the battle for human rights and human liberties and human privileges, it is the Church that is battling, almost with her back against the wall, for those very things. Youth must not be permitted to overlook that fact.

The Church is struggling to maintain the dignity of individual men. While the neopagan world is reducing man to the level of animals, or making of him gun fodder or a cog in some economic five-year plan or a servant and slave of an omnipotent and infallible state or a pawn in an international game of "swipe and grab," the Church fights for the rights of man, the son of God, the sole owner of this earth, the immortal citizen of the eternal kingdom.

While nations with dumbfounding rapidity switch to dictatorships, and fling aside their votes and their free choice, and bend weak knees to the *ipse dixit* of men who but yesterday were unsuccessful dabblers in unimportant trades, the Church is struggling for the preservation of Christian democracy.

Communism has taken the stand that men are not competent to handle so much as their pocketbooks, much less to handle even the smaller types of business. The Church fights for the rights of personal property as a guarantee of a man's freedom and an incentive for his full development.

While whole systems of education in our country and in foreign countries take the stand that parents are harmful to their children and that children should be taken away and turned over to the tutelage of the state, the Church battles for the rights of parents to love and tend and educate the children they conceived and bore.

There is more of free speech and free education and free journalism in the Church today than in most of the secular governments that brag most loudly of the freedom they grant their people.

And I have the feeling that we will do well if we build the loyalty of our young people to the Church on aspects such as these. If they see what the Church means to modern civilization, how she is struggling to save modern civilization from destruction and to push the world forward to undreamed-of heights of achievement and advance, our youth will feel differently toward her. Our enemies have lied about the Church shamefully. Those lies have been shouted in so blatant a fashion that even our young people have heard them and have been affected by them. Our answer is a vigorous presentation of what the Church has done and is doing for human dignity and human advance. And our most extravagant statements can hardly be exaggerations.

We have too often presented the Church as standing guard, as holding back, as forbidding and prohibiting, as menacing and threatening, as demanding and conserving. It is about time that we presented the Church for what it is —the embattled army of the saints in heaven and the modern crusaders on earth, both fighting for all those things that make life worth living: personal human dignity, freedom from tyranny, human rights to property and family, Christian democracy, economic liberty. It is certainly high time that we appeal to the revolutionary instinct in young hearts by pointing out that no man can be a logical Christian without praying and working with all his heart for the overthrow of evil and the establishment of the reign of Christ in the hearts of men, in society, in education, in the world of business and government and sport and entertainment— everywhere. That is revolution. We are revolutionists. We are the teachers and the breeders of revolutionists.

God give us strength for so dangerous and glorious a task!

THE LEADER

In all of our dealings with young people we are merely intermediaries. Yet we do not stand between the young person and Christ. That would be the wrong way to put it. Rather are we the ones who are to lead those young people safely to the lover of youth, the supreme captain and king— Christ.

Modern movements have in most cases been psychologically smart. They have not wasted a great deal of time in discussing issues. They have not presented elaborate platforms. Shrewdly those responsible for these movements knew that the great mass of humanity knows little of issues and doesn't take even the time necessary to read the platforms of the major candidates for a national election.

Modern movements have in every case centered around a man. For people understand a man. They love a leader.

So though probably not one Russian in a hundred would even attempt to explain communism, which he has never seen in operation and hence could hardly be expected to understand, millions of Russians walk in endless procession past the mummified body of the leader, Lenin. And from the walls of Russian houses Marx, the Moses of communism, and Lenin, the messiah, and Stalin, the Paul, look down in unholy trinity. Communism may change its face every year. It does not change the well known and propagandized faces of its leaders.

Fascism has no steady principles on which to stand. When the Black Shirts moved storm-cloudlike on Rome, no one, least of all the leaders, knew what they were coming to establish. Today the average Italian is delightfully vague about what fascism means or intends to do. But every Italian knows Mussolini. They know the man who speaks to them from his balcony in the Piazza Venezia and whips their national spirit to new heights as he compares old Rome of the Empire with new Rome of the empire he established out of the sand-baked deserts of Ethiopia.

Nazism is teutonized fascism — fascism plus a bitter hatred of the Jews and a megalomaniac conviction of German supremacy. Its foundations are as misty as those of fascism. Its principles are what its leaders feel with their ganglia after a wet Monday or a sun-lit parade of steel helmets. What difference does the vagueness of nazism make? Nazism has its central man, Hitler, and hands shoot out to greet him as he lifts the German national spirit to frenzy with an eloquence that makes empty words sound meaningful. Hitler, the man, creates the impression of a philosophy where there is only sound and fury—and personal leadership.

So communism marches in the memory of Lenin; Mussolini is the rallying figure of fascism; nazi millions mark time to the rhythm of Hitler's voice; Turkey centers its hopes in Ataturk; Austria lays its flowers and its hopes at the tomb of Dolfuss; Belgium ties its future to its new and resourceful young king; Hungary is the man Horthy; Poland is strong when it remembers the iron figure of Pilsudski; the New Deal is Roosevelt and his persuasive smile. No modern movement is simply a mass of principles and a synthesis of carefully reasoned philosophy. It is a man.

We have a man, we Catholics.

But we have sometimes grown so impressed with our carefully reasoned philosophy that we have become bad psychologists. We have forgotten the obvious fact that all men, but young men in particular, want to follow a leader. Duty in the abstract never inspires anyone. But duty to a person beloved is the strongest natural force in the world.

We have a man, the world's most attractive man—Jesus Christ.

But we have neglected Him. We have talked around Him. We have tried to inspire youth with devotion to abstract duty. We have preached the commandments. We have even thought of the Blessed Sacrament as "it," and though the neuterizing is theologically correct, it is psychologically unsound. We should have thought of the Blessed Sacrament as Christ in the Blessed Sacrament, the God-Man dwelling with us.

We have talked to the Church and have forgotten that the Church is what it is only because it is the visible body of the Savior. We have preached the principles of Christ and have forgotten to show clearly the Man whose charm and personality make those principles intelligible and acceptable. We have rambled off and gone groping into realms of the abstract when we should have clung to and should have taught our young people to cling to the hands of the charming and gracious Christ.

Christ's attitude was directly the opposite of the attitude of so many of us who teach Him. He simply said: "Come, follow me." That was the point, and the whole point. Those who served Him were to come to Him, to walk with Him, to keep Him always in sight. After they had come to Him and had learned the joy of following Him, then would He give them through the practices of His own life the principles they were to hold. But first, as He said to a hesitant seeker after truth, "Come and see." After he had seen, he would find it relatively easy to accept His principles. The charm of His life would be inducement enough to make him want to lead that life.

We have allowed frequent communion to get between our young people and Christ. This must be understood in the sense in which I mean it, but I put it that way in the hope that it may be startling. If it is, I can then explain just what I mean. When frequent communion was blessedly given by Pius X to save the world of youth from the horrible dangers that were to surronnd him during the next twenty years, many a guide of youth stood back well content. His charges were going to receive Christ in Holy Communion frequently. There was no further need to worry or to work. Christ would take care of everything. The sacrament worked *ex opere operato*. And wasn't that the guarantee of a long vacation for the rest of us?

So we urged frequent communion. The young people went to the Eucharist. They associated with Christ. But we? Well we let preparation and thanksgiving for Holy Communion practically disappear. We permitted an almost automatic reception to come into vogue. Very young children went to Holy Communion, but the extremely careful preparation that was supposed to precede the actual receiving of communion grew less significant. Let Christ do the work. We had brought the children to Him. He could now take care of them.

And all the while theologians had insisted that the grace and benefits received from Holy Communion were proportional to the dispositions of those who received. Christ could not force His graces on unwilling or distracted hearts. Holy Communion is important and always brings grace to him who receives worthily; but attentive, devout, and responsive

Holy Communion is the kind the Church wants, the kind Christ hoped for.

Does it sound odd to report that I have heard young men in conventions say flatly that they felt that communion had in their cases been too frequent? They had grown callous and careless. Their preparation and thanksgiving meant nothing. They just went and received. And I have heard the answer given by other young men: "It's not frequent communion that's at fault; it's careless communion."

And that carelessness, I believe, has sometimes got between our young people and the Christ who calls to them.

Whether or not this carelessness at communion has any connection with frequency of communion I can only surmise. But I do know that young people today do not know the man Christ. My tests of their knowledge have proved this. Early in their careers they are given the proofs for the divinity of Christ. Those proofs are later repeated, probably repeated several times. The young people know why Christ was God. But why was He man? And what sort of man was He? What sort of man is He?

Where in our educational system is there a course on the God-Man, His characteristics, His personality, the reasons that lay back of His teachings, the human motives that inspired those teachings?

When do we preach the God-Man from the pulpit? For most of us, I'm afraid, the man Christ is merely a small point of reference in our discussion of His teaching.

Priests give missions in which they thunder about sin and hell; for six nights they talk straight out of the clouds of Sinai to the accompaniment of the roar of thunder and the crash of mallet and chisel on tables of stones.

Then they end the mission with another storm around the head of Christ on Calvary. And they leave without giving the people the inspiration of that leader who alone makes the road of virtue easy and the life of goodness acceptable.

Retreat masters come to groups of eager young people, and for three days they plunge those young people into hell and parade before them a tale of all manner of sins and defects and shortcomings. Off the masters go. And the youngsters have perhaps glimpsed Christ only as the victim on the cross or the just judge come to pronounce sentence on the living and on the dead.

Yet what in the world is our religion without its founder? How can we follow a personally unknown leader? What is the Church except that Christ-born organization that speaks with His voice and utters His words and imitates and repeats His actions and carries forward His interest?

We have devotions, but we do not know to whom we are devoted. We have devotions, let's say, to the Sacred Heart, but we have no real knowledge of the Christ whose heart beat with definite interests and definite loves and—no doubt of it—definite hates. We ask loyalty from our young people, and we never really teach them the beauty and charm of the divine person, who claims and merits that loyalty. We stress a moral law and never point to the divine lawgiver, who has given us that law. We ask for an exalted Christianity, and we give our Christians only the slenderest knowledge of Christ.

The indictment is exaggerated, you say? I wish it were. Try some simple tests on your own young people, and then write to tell me how utterly wrong I am.

THE APPROACH TO CHRIST

It seems to me that our young people will be enthusiastic leaders in today's tremendous struggle for the future:

1. When they know their leader as personally as the com-

munist or fascist or nazi youths know their leaders. Christ must never be a remote and distant being. He is the man we follow. He is the man who with flying banner moves just ahead of us. He is the most real and the most alive person in all the world.

2. When they can apply to the problems of life and the problems of their own personal experience the principles of Christ. That means that they must see how Christ in His own case handled that problem. It further means that they must know what rule He laid down to meet that problem. They must know why, drawing from His human experience as well as from His divine knowledge, He laid down that precise rule.

"I always try," said a man who had succeeded a distinguished executive in a big corporation, "to think of the way in which my predecessor would have handled this or that problem. He was a man who knew what to do and how to do it. When I can see the problem with his eyes, I go ahead."

That is the spirit which each of the world's leaders of today is trying to create in the young people that follow him. It is precisely the spirit we, as leaders and guides of youth, must create in the young men and women that follow Christ.

Getting to know Christ is not such a difficult task. It means that we who are the leaders and guides of youth must deepen our own personal knowledge by prayer, reading, thinking, writing. It means that we must seriously apply the principles of Christ to modern problems and especially to the problems of youth. Any priest or religious should find that a simple and a joyous task. But even if he finds it difficult, he is fortunate enough to be surrounded by books which will give him every possible help and guidance.

The counselor or guide of young people should begin by giving intelligent talks on the man Christ. He or she (and a woman can do this as well as can a man) should discuss Christ as a man. He should show what qualities in Him made Him the leader that He was. He should discuss the historical background against which He lived and taught. For it is extremely important that our young people be shown that Christ is, not a man who dealt with a simple, primitive, almost nomadic people, but a man who dealt with a highly civilized, cynical, sceptical, alarmingly modern world. The effect of Christ's teachings on His times, the effect of those teachings through the ages can be explained against this historical background.

A whole series of talks should be given over to the revolutionary aspects of Christ: how He threw into the world the most astounding new truths; how He upset accepted standards and values; how He made war on vested practices; how He first alarmed those who held the power in politics and religion and then incurred their hatred; how, when a situation needed personal action, He acted; how He exemplified in His own life every principle that He laid down for others; how, as a result of what He taught, the world's concepts were revolutionized—concepts of property, slavery, marriage, sex relationships, women's position, labor, children, the power of the state, the rights of the individual, and so on almost endlessly.

In order to supplement these talks, which can of course be arranged in a regular series, the counselor can draw on the whole wide field of mental prayer to and on Christ. It is easy to formulate from each of our talks a mental prayer that will focus attention on the nearness of Christ and will initiate the practice of talking things over with Him man to man. And mental prayer offers limitless possibilities for intelligent development of lay devotion.

Discussion clubs concerned with Christ and His revolutionary principles are the very best type of clubs. If one discusses merely, let's say, the proofs for the divinity of the Church, or Catholic economics or sociology or history, one has a necessarily restricted field. When one starts on the personality and story of Christ, all else seems to fall into line. What He taught about the state and the rights of labor and personal importance and marriage and children—all this begins at once to become clear. That is why the intelligent leader who initiates a group of young people into the study of Jesus Christ has tapped an inexhaustible mine. The young communists who read and thrash out Karl Marx have only a primer in their hands. The speeches of Hitler can be deflated to a few ideas, most of which are either wrong or paranoiac. But the Gospels will in the hands of an interested and competent leader furnish material for years to come. Nineteen centuries of Christianity have not exhausted them. Can a study or discussion group in a matter of months or a few years exhaust them?

We have let slip a precious chance if we fail to place at least one outstanding book on Christ in the hands of each of those entrusted to us. There is the widest range of books for the widest range of abilities and tastes, everything from Mother Loyola's books for children to Grandmaison's masterpiece for the scholarly, from Papini for the sensation-loving to Fouard for the historical-minded, from St. Bonaventure for the devout to Mauriac for the modern and Goodier for the lover of beautiful prose.

And again and again the real guide of youth will come back to the simple Gospel story; he will read with his young people the glorious fullness and richness that make Matthew, Mark, Luke, and John the world's truly great biographers. Again and again he will come back to the epistles of St. Paul, who took the Gospel and made it live for his time and for all time in an application that has changed the face of civilization.

THE VOICE OF THE LEADER

Vicious is the attack made these days on the Church. "I love religion," runs the cliché, "but I hate the Church." "Christ was simple; why clog things up with an elaborate and organized Church?"

When discussing this sort of an attack with young people, my attitude is always this: The unbeliever always praises the Church for the wrong thing. I am not interested in the Church because it is a great organization. I am proud of it for its beauty and its art, but that is only incidental. What the Church means to me is identity with Christ. When I look at the Church, I see Christ. He is the head of that mystical union of which the Church is the body. And because of this perfect unity of Christ with His Church, I hear the Church speaking only what Christ spoke; I see the Church doing only what Christ did or commanded; I note the Church's interest in all the things that were dear to the heart of Christ; I perceive how those who loved Christ love His Church and how precisely the same type that hated Christ hate His Church; each gesture of the Church is Christlike; each suffering of the Church reminds me of Calvary. To me the Church is precious and important and great because Christ united Himself in perfect unity to that Church; the Church throughout all times moves at the divine impulse in perpetuation of the actions of Christ.

I believe that we will indeed forestall very much difficulty and resentment and misunderstanding if we make clear to our young people the perfect union between Christ and the Church. But if our young people become accustomed to seeing Christ over there and the Church over here, if they see Christ as a charming and attractive man, and the Church as a vigilant and dominating institution, they will perhaps love the man and dread His Church. Only after one has seen the Church in her intimate union with Christ does she assume her right relationship and proportions.

Religion for youth must be a matter:

1. Of loyalty to the known and understood person of Christ, the leader.

2. Of devotion to the Church, which as the visible body of Christ carries on His mission in the world.

RELIGION IS DULL

These two factors would be quite enough to end forever the impression that religion is even slightly dull. In itself religion is as exciting as a revolution, for it is in truth an overturning. Religion is as inspiring as the great leader can make it. It is as glorious as Christ's wonderful work, for it continues that work until the end of time.

Yet young people do find religion dull. They do later in life take this attitude: "I had so much religion when I was a youngster that I gave it up." When they are sincere in this indictment, as some of them have every right to be, what they really mean is: "I had so much dull religion when I was a youngster that it bored me to the point of leaving the Church." And the fault for that lies with us who are the representatives of religion.

In itself religion is as thrilling as Christ. It is as inspiring as the consecrated work for human souls. It is as glorious as working for the improvement and salvation of the world. It can be however as dull as the dull human beings who present it, as dreary as the grey-souled, apathetic men and women who misrepresent it.

There are deadly dull chapels and churches where people gather out of a sense of duty. When they get there, God does His part. But no one else does his. The sermon is carelessly given after practically no preparation. The members of the congregation sit and stand and kneel in sublime indifference to the great mysteries going on before their half-closed eyes. For the priests and religious in these chapels and churches have never bothered to realize that the Christian world is in the stirrings of the great liturgical movement and that the Pope has ordered lay men and lay women to pray the Mass.

With something approaching despair I go into school chapels to find that the students who a few minutes ago were full of life and bubbling with energy are now draped over the pews half-asleep and totally uninterested. But I do not despair for them; I despair for the priests and the religious leaders who are sitting comfortably in their rooms or getting ready for the tremendous trifles of geometry and English literature, when they might be leading their boys and girls in the world's most solemn act of united worship.

And I marvel at the energy that is displayed by some priests who build glorious parish churches. The construction of the churches calls for the greatest resources of architects and builders and the most generous response of the people. And then in those churches the priests rattle through a series of ill-attended requiem Masses and mount the magnificient pulpits to mumble through sermons to which they have given not even ten minutes of preparation.

If religion seems dull, it seems dull, not because God has failed us, but because we leaders of youth have expected God to do all the work.

Let's confess it with a sharp blow on our breast: We have often made religion extremely dull. Faculties and students alike have for the past ten years been shouting that religion is the dullest and least inspiring subject taught in our schools. Well if you insist, it is excellent in your school; it is some other school of which the complaint is made. The rosary is rattled off with a dull monotony that is quite stifling. The prayers after Mass are mumbled somewhere back near the tonsils. Before class or meetings dull formulas are jumbled together in a semblance of prayer, when perhaps thirty seconds of reflection might have created a mental prayer. The Holy Ghost is expected to supply the matter and the form of many a sermon and talk to young people, but even the prayer to the Holy Ghost is forgotten as the leader rises to speak.

Pessimistic? One cannot be other than pessimistic so long as even one man or one woman that is entrusted with the guidance of young people injects into the romance and the revolution which is the Catholic religion the grey note of dullness. Religion is hard, but it need never be tiresome. Religion is exacting, but it need never be unexciting. Religion makes hard demands upon its followers, but it need never fail to put its followers in the presence of the tireless Christ and to bring them face to face with truths that are beautiful and satisfying beyond the powers of man to fathom.